child

## Also by Judy Goldman

NONFICTION
*Together: A Memoir of a Marriage and a Medical Mishap*
*Losing My Sister*

FICTION
*Early Leaving*
*The Slow Way Back*

POETRY
*Wanting to Know the End*
*Holding Back Winter*

# child

a memoir

## Judy Goldman

THE UNIVERSITY OF
SOUTH CAROLINA PRESS

© 2022 University of South Carolina

Published by the University of South Carolina Press
Columbia, South Carolina 29208

www.uscpress.com

Manufactured in the United States of America

31 30 29 28 27 26 25 24 23 22
10 9 8 7 6 5 4 3 2 1

Library of Congress Cataloging-in-Publication Data
can be found at http://catalog.loc.gov/.

ISBN 978-1-64336-283-0 (paperback)
ISBN 978-1-64336-284-7 (ebook)

*Author's Note on Text:* I have used a word in two different chapters of this memoir that is deeply offensive to me and will, no doubt, also be offensive to you. In each instance, the word is part of dialogue. In one, it's spoken ironically; I've chosen to include the word there because of the context and because of my admiration for the person who used it. It also appears in that chapter as part of a thought I had as a child. In the other chapter, I included the word to convey the full horror of the moment.

For Mattie Culp
This book is *because* of you. But then,
so much that is good about my life is because of you.

*Mattie, around the time she came to work for the Kurtz
family, circa 1944. Photograph courtesy of Judy Goldman.*

# Prologue

Like thousands of white southerners in my generation, I was raised by a Black woman who had to leave her own child behind to work for a white family. At least, that's what I always believed. It wasn't until I'd written several drafts of this book, then happened upon unsettling information which had been in these pages all along, that I started asking questions of the people who were still alive. And that's when I learned there was more to the story.

A story that, of course, encompasses race. But also childhood. And all that occurs before we grasp the true scale of the grown-up world.

These are micro-narratives. Fragments that form a love story. A jumbled-up love story. The ordinary, moment-by-moment story of Mattie Culp and me—from the time I was three until her death sixty-three years later.

Memory is two parts.

First, the re-inhabiting:

*The light outside our window is fading. Mattie and I sit side by side on the edge of the bed. She takes off her glasses and places them on the Bible on her bedside table, leans closer to me so that I can rub her pillowy shoulders, mostly her right shoulder, the one that always goes stiff after a day of work. My small fingers soften the knots that need softening. She whispers, "You got magic in your hands."*

Then, the interpreting:

Our love was unwavering. But it was, by definition, uneven. She was hired by my parents to iron my dresses and fry my over-light eggs. But that doesn't begin to describe the marvel she was to me.

And what was I to her? How to be clear and un-idealized about that?

At times, I've hesitated to even talk about us. And, if I couldn't talk about us, I sure couldn't write about us. Our relationship was lovely in an unlovely context. So many contradictions. If I say one thing, I could be denying something else. My opinions might really just be assumptions, any innocence I express simply defensiveness. Nothing is ever simple.

But I've wanted to tell this story for as long as I can remember. I'm eighty now. There won't be a better time for me to get the details down. To try to understand the complications of a key relationship in my life. To answer that voice saying yes, go ahead, write our story, before it's lost.

# 1

In the beginning, Mattie and I shared a bed, a double bed that felt as wide as the world.

She came to work for us in 1944, when she was twenty-six and I was three. My sister was six. My brother was eleven. Mother was thirty-five. My father, thirty-six.

It was unusual in Rock Hill, South Carolina, for a maid to "live in." We knew only two other families who had someone actually living in the house. The pediatrician who took care of my brother, sister, and me had a live-in maid. The young widower across the street, who owned the Pix movie theater and piloted his own plane and planted palm trees in the front yard of his stucco Hollywood-like house, so different from everyone else's house—he had a live-in maid to look after his daughter. The maids who lived with these families went to their own homes on weekends. Mattie did not have her own home. Our home was her home.

I never questioned why she didn't just do day work, like other maids. Never asked her how she could just move in with a family of strangers and leave her daughter elsewhere. Never asked anything about the arrangements she'd made. I didn't know why my parents wanted someone to live in. Didn't know why we wouldn't just hire a day worker like everyone else.

I only knew this: the way Mattie wrapped her head in a faded, flowered scarf before bed, the sureness of her body beside me, her soft and generous bosom, her soft and generous everything, her quiet hymns Jesusing me to sleep.

# 2

Our room was square and airy. My side of the bed was against the wall. At the foot of the bed, a window overlooked our side yard and the neighbors' side yard, their swing set and sandbox, and farther back, their clothesline; even farther back, their henhouse, not housing hens anymore, so we used it for the plays I created and starred in and made all the kids in the neighborhood either act in or pay to see. Long, white, gauzy curtains half-hid the window but still let the light in. Mattie washed those curtains when she decided they needed washing, hung them on the line to dry, starched and pressed them on the X-legged ironing board that stayed open beneath the windowsill.

On her side of the bed, a table and lamp. Her Bible rested on a starched white doily that covered the tabletop. Beside the Bible, a small jar of the hair cream she used every night before she wrapped her scarf around her head. When she unscrewed the top of the jar, a burny smell filled the room and tickled my nostrils.

On the other side of a window that faced the front yard was a cane-bottomed chair and next to that, our dresser. One drawer held my clothes, the other two, Mattie's. Her hairbrush, hand lotion, face powder, powder puff, and small, jewel-decorated box holding her earrings were arranged neatly on top of our dresser, along with my comb, brush, and jewel-decorated box, holding my hair ribbons. Our matching jewelry boxes had been Christmas gifts from Mother one year. Mattie got ready in the morning much faster than Mother, who sat at her dressing table and put on moisturizer, foundation, powder, rouge, eyebrow pencil, and lipstick. Mattie just took off her scarf, patted her hair in place, tucking in strays, and, if we were going downtown that morning, she dabbed the puff in her powder and ran it over her face. Otherwise, fixing her hair was all she did to get ready for the day.

There was a third window, overlooking our front steps and concrete patio. You could peer down and see who had turned into our driveway, rolled to a crusty stop on the gravel, and was now ringing our bell.

Mattie and I shared a long, narrow, walk-in closet that had a small window and two extended rods holding my dresses and Mattie's white uniforms, long-sleeved for winter, short-sleeved for summer. On the floor beneath our clothes were my sandals, lace-ups, patent-leather dress shoes, and fluffy bedroom slippers, along with Mattie's white work shoes and terry cloth slippers.

On the fourth wall of the bedroom was a massive ironing machine. Afternoons, Mattie would feed fresh-washed, pastel cotton sheets through the steaming hot rollers, which she operated with her knee. Sometimes she let me sit on her lap and hold the corners of the sheet until that huge thing sucked the sheet right out of my hands, my heart somersaulting at the danger, how I had to pull my fingers away at just the right moment. A small miracle, the way those sheets went in damp and wrinkly and came out warm and smooth.

# 3

Summer evenings, after dinner and before bedtime, I'd slip into one of the crepe-paper dresses Mattie had made for me, and the two of us would take our walk around the neighborhood. In that clean light when everything green was truly green, we collected sticks and leaves and talked about the world.

I wore a crepe-paper dress because I wanted to show it off. I wanted everyone to know that Mattie and I had taken a taxi to Woolworth's on Main Street and stood at the counter for long minutes, shuffling through the packs of wrinkled paper, deciding which color to pick—chartreuse, aqua, fuchsia, or red. When we got home, we immediately went up to our room and she unfolded the crepe paper on the bed, smoothed it out with the palms of her hands, and then, leaning over, cut it into shapes only her brain knew were right. She left me sitting on the bed while she hurried out into the hall, opened the door to the linen closet, hauled back in the portable sewing machine. She pulled up our cane-bottomed chair and sewed right there on the bed. Suddenly, a skirt, a bodice, twirled straps! Layers of stiff ruffles like wings. Next, she rummaged through the top drawer of our dresser until she found her pinking shears. She handled those saw-toothed scissors like they were the tips of her fingers, nothing to it, just snip, snip, snip, and there's your zigzag hem. Finally, she held up my dress. It looked like a dance costume for an MGM musical! Something marvelous! Nobody I knew owned a dress made of crepe paper. But Mattie came up with ideas other people never even dreamed of. I wanted the world to see how she could make anything shimmery.

—————∞∞∞—————

Around the time I was four, in 1945, a tiny white frame house was being built on a narrow vacant lot on Myrtle Drive, one street over. Mattie and I watched it rise from the raw earth—the foundation, brick by brick; the house, clapboard by clapboard, eventually painted white; and finally, the roof, gray shingle by shingle. Such a cute little house. Smallest in the neighborhood, by far. A mascot house. A dollhouse.

Every time we walked by, Mattie and I stopped to assess the progress of the construction. Sometimes she said, "Don't you wish me and you could buy that house and just the two of us go live there?"

"I do, Mattie," I always answered. "I do."

Sometimes I said, "Let's just buy that house and move in."

"Suits me fine," she answered.

That house would fit us perfectly. I was not only a kid, I was small for my age. Mattie was plump, but not much taller than five feet.

Of course, I would not have wanted to leave my parents or my brother and sister. But the house was really cute. And Mattie and I would have so much fun arranging our furniture, hanging pictures, cooking meals together in the tiny kitchen.

Were we just filling the air with dreamy talk or were we saying something more urgent? If the two of us went off to live in our own make-believe, protected world, could we bypass what loomed out in the real world?

—————∞∞∞—————

We might be taking our walk.

Or she'd be tucking me in at night.

Or I'd be sitting in my father's upholstered chair at the head of the dining room table, keeping her company while she balanced on a wooden stepladder. She'd unhook each dangling crystal from the chandelier, swish it in her bucket of sudsy ammonia water, dry it with a dish towel, then hang it back where it belonged, clean and clear.

We could be doing any of the many things we did together when I would make my promise, a promise made many times over the years: "When you get old, Mattie, I'll take care of you."

Her answer, every time: "I know you will. For sure, child. I know you will."

⸎

Friends of my parents, a couple from New York City they'd met on vacation in Florida, were driving through Rock Hill and stopped off to spend the night with us. We had dinner in the dining room, my parents, the guests, my brother Donald, my sister Brenda, and I, sequined reflections from the chandelier falling over us, the meal served by Mattie on our good green-and-white china, the cream-colored linen tablecloth Mother had cross-stitched dark green, one of many she'd done. I'm sure Mattie cooked a real southern dinner for our Yankee guests—probably fried flounder, macaroni and cheese, coleslaw, steamed spinach, cornbread, caramel cake. The guests probably complimented Mattie on her cooking. I'm sure Mattie had something to say in return. Most of the meal, though, my parents and their guests talked; Brenda and Donald said a few things; Mattie served; I listened.

When I managed to get over my shyness, say a few words, answer their questions—how old I was (four), was I in school (yes, nursery school), my teacher's name (Miss Forsythe)—I sensed the two of them just staring at my face, as though they were trying to learn me, feature by feature. Any conversation that might have pressed on from there ended abruptly with my few words.

When dinner was over and Mattie was washing dishes in the kitchen and my parents and their guests were moving into the den for more conversation, I saw the woman sidle up to my mother.

First, she rolled her arm into my mother's. Then I heard her say, with her strong New York accent and a little laugh, "Judy talks just like Mattie! I can't understand a word either one of them says!"

I could have bowed down to *her* words. What they said to me: Mattie and I were a pair. We belonged together. There were identical twins in our town, the McDonald twins, and everyone always asked them if they had their own secret language. They just responded with giggles. I took that to mean the answer was yes. Mattie and I were like the McDonald twins. Add that to the list of what made us special.

# 4

If my father got even a hint of Mattie carrying four-year-old me the three long blocks to nursery school, he would straighten up to his full height of five-eleven, grow stiff as a post, give Mattie that look we all knew, and state what was obviously a fact to everyone but Mattie: "Judy is not a baby."

After I was grown, I would learn that Mattie almost quit several times during those early years because of my father's strictness, not just in dealing with his children, but in everything. He was blunt; he was stern; he was boss. There was a right way to do things and a wrong way, and it was his job to make sure everyone did things the right way. Mattie had her own way of doing things. She never openly argued with him, but I saw the expression on her face when she was sure he could *not* see the expression on her face. Despite the cranky differences between the two of them, she never left. Years later, she told me that she used to look at me and think, *Nothing is bad enough to ever cause me to leave my baby.*

As time passed, Mattie and my father developed a rock-hard admiration for each other—probably because of the goddamned (my father's word) certainty, the mechanical precision with which they each landed on facts.

One time I actually heard Mattie chide my father. They were in the breakfast room; my father had finished his corn flakes and sliced banana and was pushing back his chair, ready to leave for the store. That's when Mattie said, "You know you ain't taken no pill,

Mr. Bennie. When I counted them this morning, there was nine in there. And there's still nine in there. Now go on and take the pill."

My father took the pill.

———⊗⊗⊗———

Those mornings in 1945 and '46, Mattie and I walked up the street headed for my nursery school, side by side, her hand tightening on mine, me holding on with everything I had—until we were well out of my father's view, at least three houses away, and safe. That's when she would pick me up and carry me the rest of the way, four-year-old me floating in her arms, the two of us singing made-up songs, all full of promise.

Past the Carrolls'. Mr. Carroll owned the Pepsi-Cola bottling plant. Past Dr. Harter's. Past Mary's house, the girl everyone called retarded, who was passed along with the rest of my grade until we all graduated from high school. When Mary and I were older, we walked to school together. Past Mrs. Blakeley's, everyone's eighth grade teacher. On up Eden Terrace. Across busy Charlotte Avenue. No light there. Be careful. Past the castle-like school Donald and Brenda attended, the school I would attend from kindergarten through twelfth grade. Stand on the outside edge of the curb and wait for the light at Oakland Avenue (Rock Hill's busiest street) to turn green, then cross, enter the leafy grounds of Winthrop College, all the way back to the nursery school, which resembled a cozy little brick fairy-tale cottage, where my teacher, Miss Forsythe, whom we children jokingly called Miss So Forth, stood in the doorway, greeting students. She'd say good morning to Mattie and me. Mattie would set me down, walk me to the doorway, holding my hand. As Mattie let go, Miss Forsythe took my hand and walked me in. I always looked back over my shoulder for one last glimpse of Mattie. I usually caught her looking over her shoulder at me.

# 5

If someone came to our house to spy, they would see three children loving Mattie. And they would see Mattie returning that love. But it wouldn't take long to discover what everyone in our family knew: Mattie's and my connection was the special one.

The love between Donald and Mattie was held together by jokes. His jokes—and he knew a million—made Mattie laugh so hard she held her sides and shook. I could be upstairs and, without even cupping my ears, hear her laughter ring out from the kitchen. I could also hear her saying, "Don't make me laugh, Donald! I'm 'bout to burn this gravy!"

Brenda cooked with Mattie, the two of them spending hours deciding which recipe they would try, how they could alter it to be more interesting. Their peanut butter fudge and candy apples—the coating so hard you had to crack it over the back of a wooden chair to get it started—were famous on Eden Terrace. The little boy who lived across the street always managed to appear at our front door just as whatever Brenda and Mattie had baked was cool enough to eat.

Donald and Brenda's hearts were wide open to Mattie—all her life. And hers was wide open to them. There was no competition among us for Mattie's love. But when you start out as two beings spooned together in sleep—well, Mattie's and my connection would be hard to match.

I was a typical youngest sibling. Which meant I paid attention to and memorized everything about my brother, eight years older, and my sister, three years older.

I idolized Donald and felt sorry for him, both. Our father considered it his job to mold him into a perfect human being. Perfection would have been a son who loved schoolwork, not girls; who watched *The Ed Sullivan Show* with the family, instead of holing himself away in his room, playing his Dixieland jazz records. A son eager to work in The Smart Shop, our father's store, selling dresses, happy to spend the rest of his life in Rock Hill, eating meat loaf and mashed potato lunches at the Andrew Jackson Hotel with the men who owned shops, practiced law, and ran banks on Main Street.

Donald would never be that person. He set himself apart from the rest of us, yearning for something bigger and better than Rock Hill. He never even looked like anyone in our family. He has Mother's brown eyes and there's something about his chin that's like our father's, but nothing else from either parent. I thought he belonged in the same category as James Dean or Montgomery Clift. That air of mystery, of knowing. A level of sophistication and wit and remove.

Brenda was a different story. Everyone said she looked just like our father and was exactly like him, which meant those two tall, lanky people were forever bound in mutual admiration and understanding. If she'd been born a few years later, when girls could dream of careers other than teaching or nursing, running The Smart Shop would have been perfect for her.

She was always creating businesses that relied on her artistic talent. At ten, she spent her allowance on tiny seashells from White's Hobby Shop. Which meant *I* spent *my* allowance on tiny seashells. She turned her shells into flowers with honey-colored glue, turned those flowers into earrings and pins. Which meant *I* turned *my* shells into earrings and pins. Mother wore our jewelry. Mattie wore our jewelry. Brenda also sold her earrings and pins to

La Petite, the beauty shop we went to out on the bypass. Sometimes she allowed my jewelry to be included. La Petite was housed in an old Dairy Queen. The owner kept a display of our jewelry right by the door of the little red and white building where you came in, couldn't miss it.

Brenda and I published a neighborhood newspaper, *Eden Terrace Gazette*. She was editor-in-chief, business manager, and art director. I was a reporter. We both wrote the articles; she illustrated them. We copied each page over and over by hand, stapled them together, produced dozens of copies. It was my job to sell the papers, door to door, up the street, as far as Brenda told me to go. Mattie was always alert to my little sister status: "Judy, you've sold enough papers. You go on and do what you want to do now."

But I was awed by my sister's talents. Wanted to be with her, do whatever she was doing, learn how to *be* her. Sometimes she let me in. Sometimes, not.

The similarity between our father and Brenda—same temperament, same willful nature—meant that Brenda presented the same challenges to Mother as our father did. None of us ever witnessed our parents' quarrels, but Brenda's moods and Mother's frustration with those moods hung out there, all the years of my childhood. Brenda slammed doors. Mother pleaded. Brenda, mad at Donald, hurled an iron donkey bottle-opener at his head, missed, a donkey ear dug a deep hole in the breakfast room wall, Mother hired someone to wallpaper it over. Brenda packed a suitcase to run away from home. She even wrote a Last Will & Testament, leaving me her stuffed animals (which I didn't mind at all). Mother begged her not to go; Mattie convinced her to unpack and stay home.

I would describe my father and Brenda this way: No foolishness about them. They each projected a strength. A serious control. A certainty: I see it this way, so it *is* this way. These traits meant that my father and sister were deeply principled. But also that they were not always easy to live with.

My relationship with my father? I wanted warmth. I wanted him to be folksy. Chatty. There were flashes of warmth, and I knew in my heart he loved me, but I wanted full-time warmth. I wanted him to be Mother.

Mother was sweet-natured, affectionate, empathetic. People were always telling me, *I just love your mother!* I felt special because this person whom everyone loved . . . loved me! She didn't just love me though; she doted on me.

(Oddly, when my parents were in their sixties and Mother developed Alzheimer's, my father changed dramatically. As she slowly disappeared, he *became* her. There was then softness, where there had been the opposite.)

Donald and Brenda would probably describe our mother differently. Donald was so much our father's charge that he has very few memories of Mother, his childhood full of her absence. More than either of our parents, Mattie seemed to understand Donald's desire to go his own way. When he was eleven and needed a birthday present for Mother, he dug up an azalea bush in the Craigs' yard, two houses down, and presented it to her, stringy roots and all, wet clumps of dirt dropping all over the den rug. Mattie's face showed that she saw the resourcefulness there. My father's face did not. Mother was torn between the two.

Brenda would say Mother played favorites, that she didn't hide her partiality toward me. Not always easy for Brenda. At times, not easy for me. If Mother had been more accepting of Brenda, maybe Brenda would have been more accepting of me. But I have to admit, most of the time, I was fine with how it was.

I can conjure in my mind's eye my mother at her dressing table. She'd be wearing a pale green or pale blue silk nightgown, frilly lace neckline. I'd be wearing my teenage flannel pajamas and sitting in the flowery upholstered chair, my slippered feet on the matching ottoman. It would be evening, a dark winter sky out the windows on either side of the dressing table. Mother would have already washed her face and would now be tapping the bottle of her English Lavender lotion, getting those last drops to pool in her palm. She'd place the bottle back on the glass-topped dressing table, then rub in the lotion, hand over hand. I'd tell her that Charles hadn't called for a week, that somebody told me he was dating a girl from another school, that I was so very sad and didn't see how I would ever get over it. I could say things like that, because I had a mother whose shoulders would fold toward me, who'd reach across the space for my hands, and screw up her face to show she did not like what Charles was doing. I don't remember her exact words, but I know for sure that what she said was as soothing as the light film of lotion now on my hands.

I also discussed my teenage problems with Mattie, and she was just as sympathetic as Mother. However, I knew all about Mother's adolescence (including her boyfriends, right up until she met my father) and knew nothing of Mattie's. This was a subject I did not feel I had the right to bring up. Her adolescence, any boyfriends she might have had—all that seemed off-limits to me. Maybe it was that she never volunteered stories about her teenage years. Maybe it was that *anything* happening before our life together, in my young and unenlightened mind, simply did not exist.

———— ✺ ————

When I was born, I had trouble breathing or maybe it was that I couldn't swallow—I never really knew which. But when I was a day old, an ambulance rushed me from Rock Hill to Columbia. Mother talked the medics into allowing her to break the rules and, even though she'd given birth only twenty-four hours before, she climbed up into the back of the ambulance and held me on her lap, on a pink satin pillow, for the two-hour drive. I believe that satin pillow has found its way into every book I've written. It defines me. Because I've been resting on it my whole life. How pampered I was. Indulged.

I didn't just have the mother we all would want if we could design our own mothers; I had *two* mothers who fit that description, who acted as though everything I did was just wonderful. I was as much Mattie's as I was Mother's. But just because Mattie helped raise me does not mean Mother was absent from my life. My mother achieved something I still marvel at: She held me close, was focused on me 100 percent—and also shared me with Mattie. Mother did not miss out on a minute of mothering me; she was full-time. Yet, Mattie was full-time, too. They were totally aligned in their approach to mothering, in their tenderheartedness. Who in the world is lucky enough to have two perfect mothers, their faces forever shining down at you?

# 6

Rock Hill got its name in 1852, when the Charlotte/Columbia/ Augusta Railroad Line was being extended into the area. The depot was supposed to be located in nearby Ebenezerville, which was between Charlotte, North Carolina (twenty-six miles north), and Columbia, South Carolina (seventy-two miles south). But the citizens of Ebenezerville did not want a dirty, noisy railroad intersecting their village. So instead, engineers ran the line two miles away, over a small, flinty hill, which they marked on the map, *Rocky Hill*. A post office was built that same year, the *y* was dropped, and Rock Hill was officially established.

When we memorized the population of our town in elementary school, it was 30,000. In high school: 30,000. Years after high school: 30,000. I imagined that before someone new could move to Rock Hill, someone else had to leave or die.

We thought we had plenty to be proud of in Rock Hill. We were the fifth-largest town in South Carolina, falling right behind Spartanburg. And we had our own celebrity, Vernon Grant, an illustrator who created the characters, Snap, Crackle, and Pop, for Kellogg's Rice Krispies. He also drew covers for national magazines—*Collier's* and *Ladies Home Journal*. If you happened to pass him strolling along Main Street, puffing on his pipe, you peeked over your shoulder for a second look, happy that fame had touched our very sidewalks.

Rock Hill was a beautiful town, its lawns edged in dogwood trees, whose roots children soaked with Mercurochrome to turn the white blossoms pink. Roses climbed trellises. Maids picked camellias to float in shallow, cut-glass bowls in the center of dining room tables, when the people they worked for invited company for dinner. But right in your neighborhood, even on Eden Terrace, dead center on the sidewalk, just as you were about to step there, a snake could slither. You would scream, and a yardman (always a Black yardman) mowing the grass nearby would suddenly appear with a shovel. Even after the snake was chopped in two, the tail twitched.

This was our landscape. Camellias and snakes. The particulars of our lives. The irregular ground on which our life stories were built.

# 7

Eden Terrace was where I first struggled to understand the fixed limits on a Black person's life. Some of what Mattie suffered out in the world I witnessed; some I only heard about. And some I'm sure I was oblivious to, the way children drift above the reality that grown-ups meet head-on.

One overcast Saturday—I was probably five—I skated along the sidewalk, and Mattie half-walked, half-ran beside me, keeping up, the two of us holding hands. I loved the tingling vibration from the sidewalk through the steel wheels of my clamp-on skates, loved the skate key I wore on a string around my neck. Owning that key, even though it was just to tighten my skates, meant I could pretend I was grown-up enough to have a key to my house. Really, though, no one in my family had a key to our house. Didn't need one, since we never locked the front door.

Four houses away, Mattie and I spotted our neighbor. He was in his front yard, pushing a lawn mower, crisscrossing back and forth, one side to the other, cutting a deep pattern in the grass. Mattie called out, "Hey, Dr. Harter! How you doin' today?" (Mattie knew everyone on our street, and everyone knew her.) She stopped right then, pulling on my hand to teach me that it's good manners to pause for a moment and say hello to people. I figured I didn't need to say anything, since she'd already spoken, which was good enough for both of us. At first, I thought he wouldn't be able to hear her, and I wondered why we couldn't just keep going. But he did hear. I know, because I saw him turn toward the sound of her voice.

However, he didn't return her greeting, did not even look at her. He made a *point* of not looking at her, focusing only on me, a forced, sly grin on his square-jawed face. Then he called out over the roar of the lawn mower, "Hey, Judy!"

*Did that just happen?* I looked up at Mattie. She was still smiling her smile, so real and soft-faced. She was *there*. She was real. She was not a person anyone should ignore.

She cocked her head a little in my direction, as if to say, *All right, we can go now,* and we were off.

I wished I could have told her how that made me feel. The way my throat closed from the sadness, how I was having to work to suck in enough air. I wished I could have asked her how it made *her* feel, although I really believed I could feel what Mattie was feeling, just as she always showed me she could feel what I was feeling. My skate would work itself loose and I'd hit the sidewalk and skin my knee. She'd carry me home, pull me onto her lap, paint my knee with Mercurochrome, blow on it, stick on a Band-Aid, smooth down the curly edges, all the while murmuring, "Oh, child, that hurts Mattie so!"

I just didn't know how to tell her that what Dr. Harter did hurt *me* so.

# 8

Mattie never told me about the incident at the Greyhound bus station. I heard about it from Mother, how she'd taken Mattie to the bus station downtown and bought her a ticket to Columbia, South Carolina, to visit her cousin. Mattie and Mother walked out into the sunshine, said hello to the Black man who always situated himself between the entrance and exit, shining shoes for fifteen cents a pair, the smell of polish surrounding him. Mattie and Mother hugged good-bye; Mattie headed toward the bus, Mother to her car, where she started the engine and drove through the small parking lot. As she turned onto the street, she glanced back. In that moment, she saw the white passengers, who'd gotten in line after Mattie, nonchalantly cut ahead of her, as though they—and only they—had the right to be first on the bus to select a seat, as though Mattie wasn't even standing there, holding a ticket in her hand that cost the same as, and was identical to, theirs.

Those white passengers had every legal right to do what they did. Not only that, once Mattie was on the bus, she would have to walk to the back to find her seat. After all, it was 1948. Still, Mother wheeled around, parked, fast-walked over to the line and, in her very southern, mannerly way, patted each person on the arm, gently, almost as though they'd been friends forever, even though she didn't know them at all, and she said to each one, "Excuse me, but I believe this lady was next. Excuse me, yes, excuse me . . ." She excused-me'd those people right back to their proper places. At least, for that moment.

# 9

My parents spent three weeks every February with Mother's younger sister and her husband in a resort town called Pass-a-Grille, on the west coast of Florida, at the Hotel Rellim (Miller, the owners' name, spelled backwards).

One February afternoon in 1949, when my parents were away, Mattie and I walked up to the playground at Winthrop Training School, where I was in second grade. This particular day, we had the playground to ourselves. I climbed on the rain-rusted iron jungle gym, swung on the swings, swooped up and down on the wooden seesaw, Mattie on the far end. She kept her foot firmly planted on the ground so that she could lift me up and ease me down without a bump.

And then she said it was time to go, that the sun looked like it would set any minute, Brenda and Donald would be coming home soon, and she needed to start dinner.

"Just one more time on the jungle gym," I begged. "Please! Let me climb to the top and then we'll go."

Mattie couldn't say no to me. So up I went. To the top. I didn't care if a chilly breeze was kicking up and my dress was blowing, showing my underpants; I was loving the feeling of being so high up. My opinion was that the sun, though low in the sky, was not going to set any time soon.

But then, because the soles of my new shoes were slippery, my foot slid off that pipe and I felt myself falling, through the crisscross network of iron, my underarm catching a thick bolt where pipes were soldered together. The knobby joint ripped into my underarm, deep, to the bone. It was a wide cut. Later we'd see that it was over three inches long. And then I was lying on the hard-packed ground, breathing in the smell of red dirt.

Mattie scooped me up, pulled off her cardigan and wrapped it tight around my arm to try to stop the bleeding, ran with me across busy Charlotte Avenue, skirting cars, up the sidewalk, to a small brick house one down from the corner, breathlessly whispering to herself the whole time, "Lord, Lord." I was sobbing. My heart was thumping. We didn't know the people who lived in the house, but Mattie frantically rang their bell as though we did.

A drowsy old woman came to the door, saw the blood, my tears, Mattie's terrified face. She suddenly came to life, let us in, and, since she did not drive, called Veteran's Cab Company.

I still remember the driver's name, Lyle Whisonant. Still remember he told us he was a World War II veteran, that he'd seen a lot and he knew I'd be okay. He calmly drove us to York County Hospital. I dissolved into Mattie's lap in the back seat, she patted me, I stopped crying. Her eyes were so tightly closed, I knew she was praying.

Lyle carried me through the doors of the hospital, those strong, muscular, unfamiliar arms, and later—after I was back home—called to see how I was. For years, whenever anyone in my family took a cab and Lyle was the driver, he would talk with tenderness about the afternoon he'd picked us up, a maid and a little girl. Mattie and I always felt lucky we'd gotten him for our driver.

Once inside the emergency room, he handed me over to Mattie and said his good-byes. I settled into the arms I knew.

A nurse with a brittle smile walked over to the two of us and whispered something in Mattie's ear that I couldn't make out. The nurse tipped her head in the direction of the long hallway in front of us. I saw Mattie's face change, and then she leaned way over, unfolded my hands from around her neck, and gently lowered me to the floor. She brushed my dress so that it hung straight, and said to me, "Child, you go on now, go with the nurse. I'll be waitin' for you. You gon' be all right."

My insides clenched. But I did what Mattie told me to do and followed the nurse down the hall, holding Mattie's sweater even tighter around me. I looked back over my shoulder to catch her looking at me. But she was gone.

And so, I waited, alone, in the "whites-only" waiting room. And Mattie waited, alone, in the "colored" waiting room. I didn't know then that one thin wall separated us, a frightened woman on one side, a frightened child on the other, a child whose arm would need layers of stitches, who did not even think how the separate waiting rooms might be affecting Mattie, how it felt to her to be judged not good enough to sit in a room with a child she was certainly good enough to take care of every other day of the year, the child who only knew she wanted Mattie.

I don't remember how much time passed. I'm sure they came for me pretty quickly; they would never keep a white child waiting for very long. But they had to look for me. I'd left my room, found Mattie's room, climbed into her lap, and we were waiting there, together.

# 10

Our connected lives. Mattie and me. Our far-from-connected childhoods.

I walked the two blocks up Eden Terrace to elementary school with Brenda, or with Mary. The walk took about ten minutes, longer if we made the rule we couldn't step on a crack, longer still if it started to rain, which didn't matter as far as getting wet, just that rain meant we stopped along the way to kick the muddy water pooling in the grass beside the sidewalk. It was a very short distance if Brenda suddenly yelled, "Look out, Judy! There's a vacuum cleaner behind you!" That's when I would cut loose in fear. I believed, because I was so little, that a vacuum cleaner could suck me up. Amazing, how it might suddenly appear out in public as though that's where it did its work! I never looked back to verify. I just ran the rest of the way, leaving Brenda to enjoy the luxury of walking to school without me.

I was in love with my school, that rosy-brick castle of a building, its soaring white towers, heavily scrolled open book above the massive double front doors. Winthrop Training School was the laboratory school for Winthrop College, our state teachers' college, where seniors learned how to teach by practicing on us. In each class, we had a lead teacher and a student teacher. Our classes were small (forty-two in our graduating class—the largest ever, I believe). Every classroom had high ceilings, elongated windows looking out over wide lawns. Two playgrounds, multiple sliding boards, seesaws, swings, and that iron jungle gym. All under the shade of the spreading branches of giant oaks.

Our protected world. We were prepared for anything. Fire? We were ready. The fire alarm would sound through all three floors, bringing students into the halls to line up at the openings of the two fire escapes that twirled down the outside of the building. The excitement we felt the moment before we entered that enclosed iron chute! We were practicing for fires that would never happen, there would never be a fire in our school, oh no, we were sure of that, how safe we were, no harm would ever come to us. It was just a drill, and each of us would sit down in the dark tunnel, legs outstretched, one following another, the long glide down. Sometimes my friends and I, seeking adventure on a Saturday, met at the school, crawled up the fire escape (you needed the stickiness of sneakers or bare feet) and, with smoothed-down sheets of wax paper beneath our bottoms, hands clasping each other's shoulders, down we slid, twists and turns, faster, faster, till the last astonishing moment when our faces felt the outside breeze and our feet hit dirt.

---

I don't know how many years Mattie attended school, just that she didn't make it to high school. I don't know why she had to drop out. I do know that she could read and write. Every night, she studied her Bible. And I can picture her artistic cursive in the long, affectionate messages she wrote in the Hallmark cards she carefully selected for each of our birthdays.

I learned the history of her school while I was writing this book. Her two-room schoolhouse, Liberty Hill School, was located in the tiny town of Catawba, ten miles down a country road from Rock Hill. The wood-frame building was built in 1925, a Rosenwald school, one of many established for Black children across the South, a collaboration between Julius Rosenwald, president and chairman of Sears, Roebuck and Company, and African American educator Booker T. Washington. The Rosenwald Fund contributed start-up money to build the schools; members of the Black community raised funds or donated labor or land; local white school boards operated the schools. Those buildings had no electricity. Mattie's school had one wood stove to heat two rooms. Behind the school, an outhouse.

Since York County's economy was dependent on the cotton crop, Liberty Hill gave students time off in the spring to plant cotton, time off in the fall to pick it. Mattie told me that Black children were considered old enough to work if they could walk. She and her brothers and sisters grew up working those fields.

Liberty Hill closed its doors in 1956. I found photographs of the abandoned school online, stared at that small crate of a building. Inside, the walls were narrow boards painted white. Ceilings, tongue and groove. A dark-stained door with a transom separated each of the classrooms from its cloakroom. Records show there was a fire, which probably led to the school's closing. But it doesn't look as though much damage was done. I can still see what the school looked like when Mattie was a student.

I picture her during those frayed years, carrying books probably handed down from white schools. There she is, walking across the damp fields to the clearing surrounding the school. How far did she have to walk? Did she walk alone or with her brothers and sisters? I picture her sitting at her little wooden desk, doing her adding and subtracting with a soft pencil, maybe gazing up at the ceiling to conjure the answer, then writing down the sum, nice and straight. I see her raise her hand to be the first to spell a vocabulary word. *Good,* the teacher says. Then she raises her hand to use the word in a sentence. *Very good.* Later she'll raise her hand to ask to be excused to use the outhouse.

# 11

Her full name was Mattie Cherry Culp. Cherry was her maiden name, Culp her married name. The two of us used to joke around and say that her name was Mattie Cherry-In-The-Cup. Most anything could make us laugh.

She was married to Jay Culp when she came to work for us. They had one child, a daughter. I always knew Mattie had a daughter, that she was somewhere in the world. But where? And with whom? I didn't ask Mattie. Didn't ask my parents. I don't know whether my parents were bothered by the fact that Mattie lived with us, raising me, while her daughter was being raised by someone else. More important, I don't know how Mattie felt about her daughter being raised elsewhere, without her. Did *I* think about this daughter, worry about her? She was a fact of Mattie's life, but not necessarily a concern of mine. When I grew a little older, I knew Mattie's daughter personally. But it wasn't until I was married with children that I knew even part of Mattie's daughter's story. And then, not until recently and quite accidentally, did I learn the full story. If we can ever know all of someone else's story.

On Mattie's days off, Jay picked her up at our house to take her to his cousin's house where he lived, in Fort Lawn, out in the country. Usually, he came in for her. He'd sit at the small, round Formica-and-chrome kitchen table until her work was done. Some evenings, I sat at the table with him and kept him company, telling him the various things Mattie and I had been doing or just thinking up newsy things to say about my father, mother, Donald, Brenda, or me. I was young enough and self-centered enough to think that our lives were interesting to everyone. But, also, in that time and place, it was common among white people to assume that Black people should know everything about our lives—and be interested—and we would know very little about theirs.

Jay was a big, rough-hewn man with a gravelly voice. But he didn't talk much. Mostly, I did the talking and he nodded his heavy head and smiled slightly, never showing his teeth. If I did happen to say something funny and he had to laugh, he made sure to cover his mouth with his giant hand, as though it would be impertinent for a Black person to laugh out loud in a white person's house. His standard answer: "That's right, Miss Judy. That's right."

Sometimes, he waited for Mattie in our driveway, his old, dented-in car idling, headlights off. I often went out to talk to him. He'd roll down his window, and I'd lean against his door and make conversation as best I could until Mattie came out. She'd be carrying her overnight bag in one hand, and a brown paper sack filled with leftovers in the other.

One night—probably in the late 1940s—Jay came to the front door for Mattie. I think he must have been out-of-control drunk, because she sent him away. I didn't actually witness this, but I heard Mattie and Mother talking about it the next day.

"I wasn't about to get in that car with that man, drunk as he was." Mattie's voice was quivery. Was she crying? She and Mother were in the kitchen. I had just come in the back door. I stood in the back hall, listening. It was unusual to hear Mattie sound so sad. I was riveted.

"Oh, Mattie, you did the right thing," Mother said. "That was very scary." Even though I couldn't see the two of them, I knew she was hugging Mattie right about then.

"I ain't never goin' with him when he's like that." Still quivery.

"No, no, you shouldn't." Mother's voice sounded certain, but also a little afraid. Both, at the same time.

I went on into the den. But I couldn't stop thinking about what I'd overheard. I don't believe I knew what *drunk* meant. My parents were not drinkers—they served gin and tonics or bourbon somethings when company came for dinner, but that was about it. I did know that Jay had done something to really upset Mattie, and nobody had the right, in my mind, to do that. Not even someone who'd been such a part of our lives. Hearing Mattie's voice sound so raw made *me* feel raw.

Over the next few days, Jay began hassling her, calling over and over, even late at night. I'd be asleep, and the phone would wake me up. Mother would get Mattie up. I'd hear Mattie out in the hall, whispering into the phone on the wall, abruptly hanging up. Then I'd hear Mattie and Mother, sitting on the cedar chest that held our out-of-season clothes, beside the phone, talking quietly way into the night.

Jay then started coming around at all hours, ringing the bell, demanding that Mattie come with him, his voice rough and mean, so loud you could hear him no matter where you were in the house. Each time he came, he was drunk. Now I understood what drunk meant. I'd hear my father at the door, talking to Jay, calmly and politely, no, Mattie was not going with him, she was staying right where she was, he needed to go on home. As my father talked, he was moving Jay back down the painted-gray concrete front steps, toward the driveway. I could hear Jay arguing with my father. Arguing with my father? How could he? But my father just kept saying the same thing over and over, as he moved Jay toward his car, no, Jay, you need to leave now, Mattie is staying right where she is. The whole situation felt so strange, so frightening, so not anything I'd ever imagined could happen. Mattie's personal problems were never so observable that *I* knew about them. The only life I was aware of was the life she shared with me.

She finally asked my father to help her get Jay to leave her alone, which he did. The five of us were at the table eating dinner. My father called Mattie in from the kitchen and explained to all of us exactly what a restraining order meant, that we should report to him if we saw Jay anywhere near the house. Or if he called. I can't picture Mattie's face when my father laid out the new reality. Or anyone else's face. Maybe someone let out a long sigh. Maybe we all—including Mattie—shook our heads yes, we understood.

As far as I knew, none of us ever saw Jay again.

I don't know where Mattie went then, on her days off. Maybe to one of her sisters.

In later years, she had a boyfriend, Knox. Knox was his last name, but that's the only name I ever heard Mattie or anybody call him. He didn't talk much, but when he did, his voice was so musical you'd think he was singing. I'd say, "Hey, Knox," and he would immediately answer, without a second's pause, "Aw-right." He never waited for the other person to ask how he was; he answered the question before it was asked. He and Mattie were—what? Boyfriend and girlfriend? Lovers? Just friends? Knox would ring our bell after dinner, after Mattie had done the dishes, and she'd go out with him to his car. They'd sit in the driveway for hours, talking. Sometimes I looked out the window from upstairs and, though it was dark, I could see their heads bobbing, their hands moving, a nice rhythm, as they chatted. The car windows would be open to the warm night, rolled shut if it was cold. I wondered why they never went anywhere. I know now there was no place for those two Black people to go in Rock Hill. No restaurants or coffee shops, not even a burger joint. And going to Knox's house would've been out of the question; I knew from Mattie he lived in a house crowded with relatives.

They remained a couple until they were in their sixties, when he died of a heart attack. I didn't ask Mattie why she and Knox never married. It's the kind of question I would have felt free to ask, but didn't. The fact that it was none of my business had nothing to do with my not asking. I just assumed she and Jay never got divorced. Now I wonder if she simply made the decision she did not want another husband. My father always described her with these words: *Mattie is a person who knows her own mind.*

# 12

And how did my mother describe Mattie?

"Mattie is my best friend."

Mattie's words: "Mrs. Peggy is my best friend."

I realize this does not sound like it could be true, but this white woman and this Black woman knew each other intimately. They delighted in each other, these two compassionate, generous-hearted people, the two people I loved most in the world.

I don't believe there were many secrets on either side. I heard Mother and Mattie whisper about my father's moodiness, his stubborn nature. *Bullheaded,* Mother called it. Mother and Mattie sympathized with each other, both having to live with my father's bullheadedness. I never knew that my parents even disagreed. Because Mother had grown up in a house roiling with quarrels between her sweet mother and rascally father, she convinced my father early in their marriage that they shouldn't argue in front of the children. But Mattie saw. And Mattie knew. In a way that my brother, my sister, and I did not.

Mattie understood Mother's relationship with her husband, just as Mother had understood Mattie's relationship with *her* husband. Before Jay had appeared drunk at our house, before the restraining order, I'd overheard a conversation between Mattie and Mother, about Jay running around with other women. This intimate knowledge of each other's marriages was just one of the bonds between Mother and Mattie. They cared about each other in that way that friends are there to bear witness to the details of each other's lives.

How many times did I hear them talking, laughing, the mingling of their voices, tears, whispering, how many times did I see them touch, hug, that magnetic force between them?

I realize I'm offering a premise that seems impossible. I'm telling you that a Black woman and a white woman loved each other equally, when I know the relationship was anything but equal. Let me try to do justice to the complexity here. This white woman paid the Black woman. Mother's money bought her a cook, a laundress, a housekeeper, a babysitter. You could easily say this made the friendship less true than financed. You could say the friendship was really just mild paternalism. The white woman was the boss. It was fine for Mattie to be called *Mattie*. Not fine, in that time and place, for Peggy to be *Peggy*. *Mrs. Peggy*, that's who she was to Mattie.

Still, they shared a history. Nobody else in all the world would remember the things the two of them remembered. Of course, it was a very specific history—the history of my brother, my sister, and me. When Mattie came to work for us, Donald and Brenda were old enough to spend most of their days in school or out with friends in the neighborhood. I was in the house, at Mattie's side. I was content to be at her side, content to just sit and talk with her, to hum along while she sang, be with her no matter what she was doing. *I* was the history Mattie and Mother shared.

They also shared gratitude. Gratitude for each other.

Mattie gave Mother freedom from cooking and cleaning, the time and energy to keep the books for The Smart Shop (a part-time job she loved); to volunteer at the American Red Cross; to be "room mother" for my brother's class, my sister's, and mine; to head up her book club, music club, and garden club; to invite company for dinner; to have relatives stay with us; to play golf; and to travel with my father, all with the comfort of knowing that her children were well taken care of. Imagine being my mother! She could arrive home at six o'clock, and dinner would be ready. If she and my father were invited to a party, they just went, knowing their children would be put to bed on time. Leading up to my parents' three-week vacation on the west coast of Florida every February, all Mother had to do was take her Bermuda shorts and sleeveless shirts out of mothballs and pack her bag. No Windexing windows. Ever. No Ajaxing kitchen counters, or dusting, mopping, washing dishes, ironing. Mattie helped my mother be her best self. All those onerous and time-consuming tasks were taken care of. The benefit to me? Mother was free to just love me.

Mattie's gratitude to my mother? Her standard words: *I'm blessed.* When she unwrapped her Mother's Day gifts: *I'm blessed.* Christmas gifts, birthday gifts, cakes and candles: *I'm blessed.* Driving home from our summer vacations at Ocean Drive Beach: *I'm blessed.* In the middle of the limitless (and limited) circle we formed with her: *I'm blessed.*

Maybe it comes down to this: Those two women took good care of *each other.*

I have to wonder, though, if Mattie had not lived with us all those years, if Mother and Mattie had not lived with that intimacy, who would have been Mattie's best friend? Who would have been my mother's best friend? In a truly free world, maybe they would have found each other and formed an attachment—an attachment of equals.

But this was their situation. And they called each other "my best friend."

Even though their arrangement was rooted in discrimination, they loved each other indiscriminately.

# 13

It wasn't until I was grown, married, and living in Charlotte that I saw any blemish in the relationship between Mother and Mattie.

My mother did not know how to cook, had never even boiled water for tea. The kitchen was entirely Mattie's territory. Although Mattie was very neat and ironed in her appearance and kept our house spotless, she was not so meticulous with the pots and pans piled haphazardly in the deep cabinet beside the stove. You could hear her shoving in a pot that didn't really fit—at least, not with how the two shelves were organized. That bickering noise of metal scraping metal. Mattie did not care if she pushed a heavy cast-iron soup pot into a nonstick frying pan. Mother constantly asked Mattie to be careful when she put the pots and pans away, her words embroidered with frustration. Mattie would not answer Mother, standing fixed wherever she was, not turning to face her, not even a shift of her shoulders to let her know she'd heard. The situation was, at times, a cold persistence between them. Yet Mattie continued to arrange—or not arrange—that cabinet the way she saw fit. *Mattie is a person who knows her own mind.*

And then, in the 1970s, with Mattie having more days off, Mother finally learned to cook—but only eggs, which she fried sunny-side up for her and my father's Sunday morning breakfast. She had bought a small Teflon frying pan for this purpose and hid it from Mattie. She wanted to keep her little pan pristine. Every time Mattie discovered the fry pan, she threw it into the cabinet with the other pots and pans. And then the Teflon was scratched. That's when Mother would buy a new pan and hide it again. Mattie would find it. The whole sequence would start over.

That quick friction between them. A small splintering.

Mother complained about this to me. (Mattie never complained to me about Mother; that just wouldn't happen.) I saw both sides. And I felt impatient, as if each one were displaying a lack of virtue.

*After all, Mother, it's just a pan. What difference does it make if it gets a few scratches? Don't be so picky!*

*Why can't you take better care of the pots and pans, Mattie? Especially the one that means so much to Mother? Why is that so hard to do?*

I knew how they ought to be. I knew how they were. I never said a word, never tried to change either of them. Since it was those two, I could live with being unable to undo.

# 14

It didn't matter that we were Jewish. Easter meant baby chicks. Easter biddies, we called them, dyed lime green, pink, lavender, or powder blue. Every year, Mother drove Brenda and me to the outskirts of town to Rock Hill Feed & Supply, where we selected our chicks. Just like all our Gentile friends.

Jewish/Gentile. Observed Easter/didn't observe Easter. Believed Jesus was resurrected from the dead/didn't believe Jesus was resurrected from the dead. None of that mattered to Mother. She focused on the part of each holiday she considered fun. Easter? Oh, let's go get ourselves some biddies!

In 1949, I was seven and couldn't decide between pink and blue. Brenda always chose lavender. Every year, lavender. Even at ten, she knew what she liked. Lavender was her trademark color. She even clipped a photograph from *Good Housekeeping* of a bedroom with lavender walls, pasted it in her scrapbook and wrote beneath it, white ink on black paper: *my dream bedroom.*

Rock Hill Feed & Supply was housed in an old building, a former cotton mill. The owner was the father of a friend of mine; they lived one street over, on Milton Avenue, next door to my uncle and his family, my father's older brother. Rock Hill Feed & Supply sold every product Purina made—not just dog and cat food: "feed and seed." They also sold whatever a hardware store sold, hammers, nails, mailboxes, light bulbs, wheelbarrows. Also fresh eggs from local farms, summer vegetables, homemade jelly, molasses, and country ham. Next door was a cotton gin. Across the street, they sold coal. Rock Hill Feed & Supply smelled like hay, like dry grain, like the fertilizer they sold in giant, floppy bags. It smelled like mulch, although I wouldn't have known what mulch was then.

I knelt beside the large wooden box that held the baby chicks, rolling about in the sawdust, their awkward fluttering. I picked up a pink one, put it down, picked up a blue one. When Mother saw that I was having a hard time deciding, she said, "Would you like to have two?" Typical of her. Nothing should ever cause me a minute's anguish in this sweet life of ours. If having to decide which chick I wanted was perplexing, then let's just eliminate the problem. Get two. Her favorite expression: "Don't push it." She wrote my sister and me excuses from school if we were tired. "You don't need to work so hard," she told us. "*B*s are just as good as *A*s." If we were sick, she brought us the meals Mattie cooked on a pink wicker bed tray. Anyone would love to be sick in our house! Aunts stayed with us when they were recuperating from surgery. They called our house "Kurtz Rest Home." Sometimes there'd be a tiny vase on the bed tray, holding a zinnia from the yard or a couple of pansies. We had special pastel-blue-and-white "sick china," decorated with a delicate rose in the middle, the dinner plate smaller than normal. Mother believed that when you don't feel well, food is more appetizing on a half-size plate.

———※———

Brenda's lavender chick died the next morning. She was sad, for a moment, but then carried on with her life. She was practical like that.

Both my chicks lived. And lived. By summer, they had grown into full-sized—surprise!—roosters. They strutted around our fenced-in backyard like kings. They were my pets, like other people had dogs. I carried them up and down the sidewalks of our neighborhood, showing them off, one under each arm, as though they were prizes I had won. I honestly believed they knew their names, because when I called, they came. Looking back, I realize it was the glassy kernels of corn I scattered in the grass that they came for. But when they were scratching around at my feet, I gave them plenty of praise for their intelligence and loyalty.

One night in late summer, a storm blew in. This was no ordinary storm; it was a welter of pounding rain and wind, lightning and thunder, purple-black skies.

I was sitting at the dinette table in the kitchen, chatting with Mattie while she finished the dinner dishes. I turned to look out the window, and, as soon as my eyes adjusted to the dark, I saw my roosters scooting around in what was now a very muddy yard. They were obviously scared to death, trying to find a safe spot.

Under the forsythia bush beneath the kitchen window? No, not safe enough. Bunched up against the side of Brenda's and my white wood playhouse? No protection at all. Those poor animals were hopping all over the place, frantic.

I immediately went into the den, where my father was reading the newspaper.

"Can we bring my roosters in?" I asked. "Just for the night? They hate being out in this weather."

"Roosters don't belong in the house" was his answer. He never even lowered his paper. "They'll be fine right where they are. Just fine." He added that last part under his breath, but loud enough for me to know the subject was closed.

I went back into the kitchen. Sat at the table. Stared out the window. Couldn't even find my roosters now.

Mattie turned off the water, gave the faucet an extra twist, looked over at me. She knew what I was thinking. Maybe she'd heard what I'd said to my father.

"They're so scared," I said, just to drive home the point.

"I know," she said, drying her hands on a dishtowel, then finishing the job on her apron, a flowered one she'd sewn herself. "Let's wait a little bit. We'll figure it out."

That night, late, I felt her light touch on my arm. By now, my parents had added a new master bedroom and bath, and Brenda and

I shared their former room. Donald kept his room. Mattie had her own.

I opened my eyes and saw that Mattie was standing beside my bed, an expression on her face I couldn't make out in the dark. She was still wearing her uniform and apron. Brenda was sound asleep in the twin bed next to mine.

I sat up, rubbed my eyes, saw that Mattie was holding an umbrella, folded up. She helped me out of my covers, cocked her head that I should follow her to the landing. I stayed close behind, down the stairs, through the back hall, to the screened-in porch (really, just a tiny utility room).

Rain was blowing in through the screens. She reached over the wooden crate of Coca-Colas on top of the clothes dryer, rummaged through the tool cabinet on the wall, found a flashlight. Then she clomped out into the muddy yard, raising her umbrella at the same time. I watched through the screen door. It was raining so hard I had to lean forward to keep her in sight, my face pressed to the screen. I could taste the aluminum. But where were my roosters?

Mattie hitched up her skirt a little and leaned under the hydrangea bush, shaking the branches gently until the blooms fell around her, in the flashlight's glow, like blue stars. Then she trudged over to the whitewashed stones lining the flowerbeds and tipped a big one to see if a rooster could be hiding behind. Her flashlight flung strips of light everywhere.

She threw her light to the back of the flowerbed. There were my roosters, huddled together near the hedge. She threaded her way through the flowers and reached down and scooped up both roosters. How she did that and held on to her umbrella and flashlight, I don't know. But just as a suck of thunder made me clap my hands over my ears, she opened the back door and brought my pets in, letting the wet umbrella and flashlight drop to the floor in the corner.

She didn't say a word. She headed into the hall bathroom, took a towel from the laundry basket on top of the washing machine, and dried the roosters off as best she could. Then she carried them into the kitchen, with me following close behind. She carefully eased each one down onto the linoleum. They just sat where she'd put them, clustered so close together they looked like one very plump rooster. I waved good night to them and followed Mattie out of the room.

With her foot, she closed the swinging door between the kitchen and back hall. Then she went through the dining room, through the breakfast room, to shut the other door leading to the kitchen.

I followed her up the stairs. Her white work shoes left little puddles on each step. Her white stockings were shiny damp. I hated that she'd put herself in danger, hated she had to be up so late, hated she'd gotten so wet. But I was relieved my roosters were safe.

While we slept, the storm came to an end.

The next morning, just as the sky began to lighten, loud squawks filled the house. My father, mother, Donald, Brenda, Mattie, and I all jumped up—probably the same minute—and stumbled sleepily down the stairs, my father in his loose cotton pajamas and leather slippers taking the lead. Mattie and I knew what the noise was. The rest of the family had no idea. The squawks were clearly coming from the kitchen.

My father pushed open the door. At first, all I could see was a stir of red and brown. My roosters were skittering around, flying as high as their fat bodies would allow, up onto the counters, back down again, almost to the counters, down, then up on the counters. Big swoops. Wings. Feathers. Beaks. Scaly feet.

When I finally was able to focus on something other than my roosters, it looked as though everything that had been on the counters was on the floor and whatever was breakable had broken: the cookie jar, iced tea glasses from last night's dinner left to dry on a dish towel, the ceramic canisters that held sugar and flour. So much sugar and flour everywhere, you'd think it had snowed inside.

I didn't dare look at my father, but I could sense the stiffness in his back.

"*Goddamned roosters,*" I heard him mutter.

Brenda stood close to him. I put one hand on Mattie's back, the bumpy ridges of her chenille robe soft beneath my fingers. My other hand held onto Mother's arm, her cotton sleeve. I don't remember whether Donald was still standing there with us or had already gone back up to bed.

Then, as though Mother, Mattie, and I had actually discussed and decided to do this thing together, the three of us knelt at exactly the same instant and began picking up broken glass—the icy needles, the larger pieces curved like shells.

"I'm sorry 'bout all this, Mrs. Peggy. Judy was worried about her roosters," Mattie said, doing a little head nod my way. "I couldn't stand to see that."

"I know, Mattie," Mother said, patting her shoulder. "It's okay. You were very sweet to go out in that awful storm and get them."

We went back to picking up glass. My roosters were now just walking around the kitchen, nervous.

When I saw in Mother's and Mattie's faces that they were worried I might cut myself, I stopped helping and gathered up both my roosters in my arms to try to comfort them. I could see through the windows that the sun was making its way up over the back hedge and higher.

My father took one of my roosters from me, and Brenda followed his lead and took the other; they carried them outside. I stayed with Mother and Mattie in the kitchen as they stacked the rest of the broken glass in tall, teetery mounds in the palms of their hands. Then I heard my father and Brenda heading back upstairs to bed.

---

Mattie had a friend named Vermell, who lived out in the country. Vermell had actually been the person who'd introduced Mattie to Mother back in 1944. She had worked for my parents for years. She did the laundry and cleaned the house but did not like cooking and was not crazy about children. Mother was looking for someone who could do it all—clean, cook, do laundry, take care of children. Mattie was that person.

Vermell agreed to take my roosters, promised to keep them alive and not kill them for any reason. Mother, Mattie, and I drove out to visit them several times over the coming months. Roaming freely in Vermell's dirt yard, they appeared well taken care of. I didn't know for sure, of course, but they seemed content.

What I did know for sure: Mattie would trudge through mud for me. She would go to the ends of the wet, pulpy earth to keep this child happy.

# 15

Rock Hill was no different from any other town in the South in the 1940s and '50s. We had our side-by-side "white" and "colored" water fountains in our hardware stores, drug stores, five-and-dimes.

We had our swimming pool at the YMCA, open to all. Except half the town's population.

Our family doctor's office had a "whites only" waiting room, as comfortable as any parlor, tufted sofa and chairs, antique clock, damask drapes—walled off from the "colored" waiting room, bare as a jail cell.

At school pep rallies and Friday night football games, we stood when the band played "Dixie," a song that felt as patriotic to us as "The Star-Spangled Banner."

In our school's May Day celebration, the girls and boys in my grade sang and danced around the Maypole to "Jump Jim Crow," having no idea it had been sung in the early 1800s by white minstrels in blackface, mocking the enslaved.

> *Jump, jump, jump, Jim Crow!*
> *Take a little twirl and around you go.*
> *Slide, slide, and step just so.*
> *Then you take another partner,*
> *And you jump Jim Crow!*

I know now that the song was based on an African folk tale involving a crow named Jim, who appeared foolish but got what he wanted through clever maneuvers. Enslaved people sang and danced to the song, sometimes even adopted a Jim Crow attitude (playing dumb) in an attempt to avoid harsh labor. Eventually, of course, the term *Jim Crow* referred to segregation laws in the South.

My friends and I saw MGM musicals at the "whites only" Pix Theater. We watched Esther Williams swim in her tight little rubber bathing cap and waterproof lipstick. We saw Doris Day sing and cry and sing, Ann Miller tap as though she invented the Morse Code. The Pix was also where Mother, Brenda, and I saw *Gone with the Wind.* We sobbed over Melanie. And Ashley. We did not sob over Margaret Mitchell's romantic and distorted view of the South, did not even think of it that way. Mother had only one Kleenex in her purse, and we passed that tissue among the three of us until it was shredded. The Pix Theater was tucked in among the columned homes on proper Oakland Avenue. These homes had gardens front and back, thick willow oaks. The Pix was pure Hollywood glamour —smooth stucco, modern—just like its owner's home across the street from us. The trees outside the Pix were the opposite of willow oaks; they were palm trees imported by Bob Bryant (even his name sounded like a movie star), who regularly flew his private plane to Hollywood, where he knew famous people. At least, that was the rumor. The Pix was one of the few places in town that had air-conditioning. It also had velvet seats, which, when you sank down, sighed *luxury.* This ultramodern, glitzy theater did not fit in that historic, well-bred neighborhood, but it was so top of the line, no one seemed to mind.

The Stevenson Theater, near the bottom of Main Street, just before it dead-ended into Trade Street, was not glamorous—sticky floor, lumpy seats. And it admitted whites *and* Blacks. White customers sat downstairs. Black customers climbed a steep, metal, outdoor stairway to the dark balcony. I couldn't see into the balcony from where I sat. But I knew people were up there, eating popcorn, watching the same movie I was watching. Sometimes I could hear them. I wondered if, when it rained, they had to sit through an entire movie, soaking wet.

My father's twin sister and her husband owned the Carver The-ater, the "colored picture show," across the railroad tracks, where Main Street and Black Street met. The Carver had originally been a Quonset Hut. It now had a tacked-on façade that was a caricature of a swanky Hollywood theater. Peeling stucco. Yellow as corn on the cob.

One summer evening, around 1950, Uncle Morris took his youngest two children and Brenda and me to the Carver. Our fam-ily was not close to their family, after a falling-out my father had with my aunt and uncle over money and ethics. Their family lived only a few blocks away from us in our small town, but my head-strong father would not speak to his twin sister. Mother still did nice things for them, like remember their birthdays and take them soup if somebody had surgery. She also pleaded with my father to reconcile with his sister. But that was not going to happen. Their family seemed fine to me. Two of my four cousins attended my school. Uncle Morris seemed especially fine, because he played the organ on the Shriners' float in the Christmas Parade. To me, he was Rock Hill's version of a rock star.

I don't remember how it happened that Brenda and I were with our uncle and cousins one night at the Carver. Don't remember what movie we saw. I do know we sat in the projection booth, door closed, so protected. For sure, we didn't mingle with the regular customers who'd paid to see the movie. That would never happen in South Carolina, white children sitting beside Black grown-ups.

The other thing that would never happen: Mattie seeing a movie at the Carver. That would have been "beneath" her. There was a sense of refinement about her—maybe as a result of living on Eden Terrace, maybe innate. Of course, she could not buy a ticket to the Pix, but she would rather not see movies at all than sit in a theater that was not clean, not up to her standards. "You think I'd go down there? In that neighborhood? With that rough crowd?" she said to me once, when I asked if she'd ever been in my uncle's theater. "I wouldn't set foot in that place."

—⊷⊶—

When the five of us arrived at the Carver and passed the line of customers waiting outside to buy tickets, I didn't think I had the right to stare, so I kept my eyes straight ahead. Which took so much energy, my stomach hurt. Finally, I looked at those people, lit by the setting summer sun, fanning their faces with their hats or handkerchiefs. At one point, my eyes met a girl's eyes (she was about my size), and I smiled at her as if to say, *For sure, I'd like you if I knew you.*

My uncle did not take us into the auditorium. But I could glimpse it as we walked down the long hall to the stairway. I had to work hard not to notice how oven-hot it was—only one breathless floor fan on either side of the stage. Then up the stairs to our private perch. Lord, I could've been in the movies myself, the way I was acting as though the entire situation—our two families, the falling-out, the way some people separate themselves from others—as though all that was completely normal.

# 16

Every afternoon, when time began to weave itself down, after they'd finished their vacuuming, mopping, and dusting and before they needed to start supper, Mattie's friend Pernettia, who worked for the O'Neals in the big white house on the other side of the hedge, would burst into Mattie's bedroom, where she was finishing her ironing and I was sitting on the edge of her bed, keeping her company.

Pernettia didn't need to ring our bell or knock on the door. She was probably the only visitor to our house who walked right in. She just unlatched the gate in the hedge, crossed our back yard, opened the screened door, then up the stairs to Mattie's room.

Adults I knew would probably have said Pernettia "talked like a white person," and, unlike most maids in those days, she was able to continue her education. Mornings, she worked toward her degree in elementary education at Clinton Junior College, a historically Black Christian college in Rock Hill. Afternoons, she took the bus to the O'Neals', where she cleaned house and took care of their three children.

She would plant herself in Mattie's doorway, hands on her hips, head cocked, eyes on Mattie, and say, with more than a hint of mischief and irony in her voice, "You just the nigger I been wantin' to see!"

The two of them would practically fall over laughing. I laughed, too. I always laughed when the two of them laughed. But my feelings were mixed.

First, there was the shock, the pain of hearing graceful Pernettia utter that word. I knew plenty of white people who used the word, but never anyone in my house. And certainly not Pernettia. So hearing her say it, out loud, in the room at the top of our stairs, took my breath away.

I have to add, typing the letters on this page takes my breath away. I am so fearful of offending. Fearful of appearing callous. But even expressing that fear is pulling the spotlight away from the many-pronged word and turning it on myself. *Look at me! I'm so enlightened!*

But there is an overriding story here. That word was the whole point. Pernettia, a person who would normally never use it, was expressing something basic about the system she and Mattie were victims of. She was even going so far as to mock it.

Maybe even using it as a term of endearment.

Which is why Pernettia's remark made me feel left out. All that affection and familiarity between the two of them. Their shared scorn of the word. Nobody would ever say to me, "You just the nigger I been wantin' to see." I was clearly not one of them, even though there was nothing I wanted more than to be right in the middle of their camaraderie.

I also wondered if Pernettia was Mattie's best friend. Instead of Mother. In those shaky minutes when I was not sure where Mattie's loyalty lay, I decided—just to reassure myself—that it was possible for her to have two best friends.

Still, I loved when Pernettia came, loved hearing them talk and laugh, loved seeing their friendship up close, loved that it was *our* house they chose for their visits, wondered if two Black maids would even be allowed to visit in any other house in the neighborhood.

# 17

Early evening, here's where you'd find me: sitting at the little round table in the kitchen, where I could look out over the backyard, our two striped canvas hammocks, flower beds, their blousy pastels, all the way to the bushy privet hedge. But I wouldn't be looking out the window. I'd be watching Mattie at the sink, cutting up yellow crookneck squash for her famous squash casserole, her quick hands flicking the small knife. I'd watch her take a step over to the stove and cock the lid on the rice to make sure it wouldn't boil over. Then she'd lift each bony piece of chicken from the iron skillet, chicken she had brined in salt water, dipped in buttermilk and flour, fried in hot Crisco. She'd place each crispy leg, breast, thigh, wing, and liver on a brown paper bag torn open and spread out over the counter. She ran that kitchen like a magician doing a plate-spinning act. I paid close attention, watching the grease from the chicken darken the paper in wider and wider circles. I would have been happy to spread myself over that whole room. I thought of it as our private place. Everything right. I loved how warm it was in winter, cool in summer. The *tk-tk-tk* of grease popping in the pan, the smell of a pineapple pie (her invented recipe) cooling on the counter, the browned breadcrumb topping on the squash casserole she pulled from the oven, steam clouding her glasses, a dish towel grabbed hurriedly to substitute for the potholders she didn't have time to find in the drawer. Mattie and I would be talking, the beginnings of my learning how to have a grown-up conversation. There were times, though, we didn't talk, when Mattie sang her hymns and I hummed along.

She did not sit and eat at the table with my family. Mattie cooked, Mattie served, we ate, we said how good everything was (could she even hear our compliments?), Mattie cleared the table, Mattie washed and dried and put away the dishes. While the five of us ate together, she ate alone at her table in the kitchen.

Did her absence at our table even register with any of us? The abnormality of what then seemed so normal?

---

The story goes that I was such a slow eater, I ate my green peas one at a time. The rest of the family would finish dinner, then leave me alone at the table, my father's instructions that I had to finish everything on my plate. I'm sure my mother did not agree with my father's rule, but she would never have confronted him. At least, not in front of us.

How quickly, though, the hard edge of loneliness vanished: Mattie would come and sit next to me, the only time she ever sat at our table. She'd encourage me to eat what I could and just leave the rest, her arm, perfumed with cooking smells, around my shoulder, her face inches from mine, my heart pudding.

---

Years later, after my parents died, my husband, Henry, and I would drive from Charlotte to Rock Hill to bring Mattie back to our house and, together, she and I would cook Thanksgiving dinner (well, she cooked, and I chopped or stirred whatever she told me to chop or stir). There would be ten of us—Brenda, her husband Chuck, and their four sons, Henry and me, our daughter and son—and we would beg Mattie to sit at the dining room table with us. She always made excuses. "I'm so full from tasting everything while I cooked, I can't eat a thing." Or "I got some things I need to do in the kitchen. Y'all go on and be together."

On less formal occasions, just an ordinary supper, she would join my family of four at our pine table in the kitchen—the only time she sat down with any of us for a meal. I don't think she ever ate with Brenda's family at their table. I was her baby, and if she were going to sit and eat with anybody, it would be me. Don't think I didn't cherish my treasured spot.

When Mattie was in her eighties, she was still cooking, but not the elaborate meals she'd once cooked. Every now and then, I roasted brisket, potatoes, and carrots—her favorite, which my grandmother (Grandma Kurtz) had taught her how to make and she'd taught me. "Cooking Jewish," Mattie called it. I'd cart my Pyrex casserole in the insulated carrier she'd given me for my birthday to her house in Rock Hill. We'd sit in her dining room, lace placemats, flowers from her yard in the center of the table, the pretty things Mother had given her—ceramic figurines, vases, crystal goblets—all displayed behind glass in her china cabinet.

But would she sit with us at a big holiday meal in the dining room at my house or my sister's house? Absolutely not. Mattie, who otherwise denied me nothing, refused to join us, no matter how many different ways I proposed it. I suppose sitting at the table with us would have disrupted too many long-established patterns. I suppose we just could not calculate or understand the discomfort she would feel if she had to change what we'd all considered normal our whole lives. Her view from the dinette set in the kitchen of the house I grew up in—that narrow doorway leading into the breakfast room. We just don't know how deeply imbedded separation can be.

---

Thanksgiving, late 1990s. Again, Mattie sat at the table in my kitchen, while Brenda's family and my family sat, all together, in the dining room, eating the turkey and cornbread dressing, rice and gravy, sweet potato casserole, green beans, ambrosia, and pies Mattie had prepared. Each of us left the table at various times to go sit with her for a while in the kitchen. But she would shoo us back, saying she wanted to close her eyes and rest a little.

Halfway through the meal, a friend of ours dropped by. He and his wife and Henry and I had been to a restaurant a few nights before and taken each other's credit card by mistake. He came to return our card and pick up his. (When we'd first discovered the switch, we joked about what we'd already bought with the other's Visa—a new car, airline tickets to Australia.) Thanksgiving evening, when our friend popped in the back door, he encountered Mattie alone at the kitchen table and, this many years later, still has not stopped teasing me. "Oh, so liberal you are, Judy! Poor ol' Mattie sitting alone in the kitchen, white family in the dining room!"

I try to laugh along with him, but my laugh comes out slightly fake, because something opens up inside me and I want to say, *No, no, you don't understand. You need to know our whole history, that Mattie and I were special, what you saw is not how it was, you're categorizing us and I don't want anything about Mattie and me to be categorized.* I want to say . . . I don't know what I want to say. If I could come up with what I want to say, I wouldn't need to write this book.

# 18

Yes, we recited prayers in hushed voices over crayon-colored Hanukkah candles. And yes, Mother invited Brenda's Girl Scout troop and each of our grades—my brother's, my sister's, and mine—to light the Hanukkah candles with us. But throwing shade over the menorah in our den was a very tall Christmas tree, silvery with tinsel icicles, heavy with satin balls. Our house was *so* decorated (pearly mistletoe dangling from light fixtures, garlands on the mantel, poinsettias), we were a regular on the Rock Hill Christmas Tour of Homes.

Why would a Jewish family celebrate Hanukkah *and* Christmas? I'm sure we were the *only* Jewish family in Rock Hill who did anything for Christmas. Blame it on my mother's exuberance. And that belief of hers in celebrating whatever there was to celebrate. She and Mattie spent days getting the house ready, one on a ladder hanging mistletoe, the other bringing in pots of poinsettias from the car, both working at straightening the tree, one tilting branches, the other standing back to gauge.

Christmas Eve, my parents closed the store late, marked down clothes for the after-Christmas sale, hosted a party for the salesladies and their families, then headed home to create Christmas for Donald, Brenda, Mattie, and me.

Mattie went to bed early. "Makes Christmas mornin' come faster," she always said. Donald was out with friends or in his room listening to his records. Brenda and I read our movie magazines under the brass floor lamp separating our twin beds—until we heard our parents bringing in packages from the car. Then, quick, lights out.

Just before daybreak, when the sky was charcoal and the stars were as bright as they would be before giving in to the first light of morning, Brenda and I scrambled from our quilts into the chill of the room to take a quick look out the window. If the O'Neals' lights were on, which meant they were up (they always were), we knew we had a case for rousing our parents and Mattie and Donald. The rule was, nobody could move toward the stairs until everyone was ready. Which meant Brenda and I sat on the top step waiting. She dared me to venture down. I dared her. We sat there. Finally, in a line, we all headed down.

Presents filled the den. Mine were tucked around my small desk in one corner. Brenda's around her desk in the opposite corner. Donald had the upholstered wing chair. Mattie, the red leather loveseat. Mother and Daddy, opposite ends of the brown leather sofa. We each received one main gift from Santa, and lots of smaller ones from everyone in the family.

One Christmas, Mattie's big gift was a diamond ring. I can still see her opening the tiny, navy-blue velvet box, how she slipped the ring onto her finger, held her hand up to the light, flipped her hand back and forth so that we could all see how the ring was shining, shining, as though that stone had been mined just for her. And, through it all, her laughing voice: "Lord, Lord, looka' here! Just looka' here! We are truly blessed!"

I know her excitement was the exact reaction Mother had envisioned when she'd wrapped the box in silver foil. Mother always wanted to give gifts you did not expect. Way beyond your dreams.

Mattie wore that ring until the days she was softly dying, too sick to know what I was doing when I slid it off her finger. It was easy to take the ring off; she had lost so much weight, even her fingers were thin. I stored it in my pajama drawer, knowing to whom it should ultimately belong. That ring: one solitary stone, perfect in its cut ripeness, a particular shade of brilliant.

Year after year, we were steeped in what went on in that room Christmas morning, wrappings and ribbons, so early, the sky outside the windows still charcoal, everything inside silvery. But in the end, it's all just memory.

# 19

There was a girl in my grade all through school, Ann, who lived with her parents, her sister and four brothers in a rickety house with a sagging roof on the Winthrop College farm. The top of Eden Terrace ended at the picture-perfect campuses of Winthrop Training School and Winthrop College. The bottom of Eden Terrace ended at the farm. Ann's father and, I suppose, her brothers worked that land. Because our school was part of Winthrop College and therefore private, we students were not only white; we were firmly middle- and upper-middle class and college-bound. Many of my classmates' parents were Winthrop College professors. Ann and her siblings were the poorest white people I knew, for sure the poorest students in our school, probably able to attend because their father was employed at the farm.

Ann always seemed just a little bit sad to me. It was around fifth grade—1951—when I began to wonder if there was something I could do to help her be happier. When I told Mattie my thoughts, she came up with the idea of inviting Ann to our house one afternoon after school for a makeover. That would surely make her happy. Mattie would wash and style her hair, maybe even give her a haircut. Just a trim to perk things up. Then she would iron Ann's dress, make it look fresh. Or the three of us might take a cab to Main Street, and Mattie and I would buy her a new dress.

I did end up inviting her over. But we just played in my back-yard playhouse with my collection of stuffed animals. When we took a break and came inside, we sat at the table in the kitchen and drank tall glasses of Mattie's lemonade and ate her chocolate chip cookies. Mattie talked with Ann and me some. But neither Mattie nor I knew how to broach the subject of the makeover. So the afternoon passed, and then it was time for Mother, who knew nothing of the plan, to drive Ann home.

Even though Mattie and I did not accomplish what we'd mapped out, we never stopped fantasizing how we might help Ann look better. But it wasn't just *this* Ann. There were other Anns in town we wanted to bring home and fix up. It was one of our pet topics: Who we could help live a better life.

Mattie and I would be walking down Main Street, usually on our way to one of Rock Hill's three five-and-dime stores. We'd pass a white woman, obviously poor, needing fresh clothes, new shoes, a haircut.

"We could do somethin' about that," Mattie would whisper to me.

"Wouldn't take much," I whispered back.

I had no idea how patronizing—cruel, really—we were being. Mattie, I am sure, would never have seen our scheming as anything but generous and caring. It's just that, together, we thought we could solve some of the world's problems. A Black woman and a white child, a little bit snobbish in our imagined specialness. Could she have possibly been as unaware as I that all of us were stuck in our particular positions in society, that Ann and the woman, being white, were higher up the ladder than Mattie? And did we really think a haircut could change a person's life? I probably believed that the bond between Mattie and me lifted her all the way up to my family's rung. Wasn't our mutual love enough to override the barriers that kept her in her place? Couldn't the two of us help poor white people override their own barriers, lead happier lives? Look better?

# 20

It wasn't just poor people Mattie wanted to help look better. At times, she thought *I* needed a makeover.

"Lord, child, look at how everybody else is dressed so nice! And you, just in your sweater and pants!" That's Mattie, in 1979, looking at a snapshot taken at my thirty-eighth birthday dinner, my girlfriends and me, little bowls of wonton soup steaming, all of us around a table in a downtown Chinese restaurant. Mattie was right. The other women were wearing dressy clothes—one, a silk blouse with a scalloped neckline, others in dresses or fancy sweaters. And yes, I was wearing a basic gray turtleneck sweater and basic black pants. Like something you'd run errands in.

She was critical of my housekeeping, too.

"Looks like nobody lives here," she declared more than once, running her finger over an end table's surface or pulling on her sleeve to rub smudges off a windowpane. I'd brought her to my house for some occasion, and she'd begun her assessing.

"You think these string beans are worth cookin'?" Her evaluation of the beans I'd bought for Thanksgiving dinner, which the two of us were snapping into a colander in the sink. She held up a shriveled bean, let it flop over, wriggled it a little to make sure I saw how past-due it was. I dried my hands on a dishtowel, tucked my purse under my arm, and headed to Harris Teeter, hoping to do better with a different sack of beans.

She never sounded stern. But there *was* the edge of judgment in her voice. And her jaw muscles were working. There was also an upward turn to her lips, as though she were saying, *Isn't this funny? Me telling you, a grown woman, what you're doing wrong!*

I do believe the lip curl was saying just that. Not: *Isn't this funny? Me, a Black woman, telling you, a white woman, what you're doing wrong!*

My reaction: It's not like I had discovered my face on a wanted poster. This was Mattie. And if I could still learn from her, well then, good. Outwardly, though, I offered up excuses:

"But my sweater is *brand new!*"

"Things just get so dusty lately. I don't know why."

"These are the best beans they had. I was so careful picking. Really."

Secretly, I was grateful there was someone who loved me so much that she cared how I looked, cleaned, and shopped.

But why did she do it?

Maybe she thought she had to pinch-hit for my mother, who was now in a nursing home and not able to talk or walk or recognize anyone. All those years, Mother had counted on Mattie to look out for me. Maybe Mattie was just making good on her word.

Maybe she felt that how I conducted myself was a reflection on her. If I dressed well, if I kept my house clean, if I knew a good green bean from a bad green bean, she had raised me right.

# 21

The town I grew up in was quiet and calm and civilized, as though everything within the Rock Hill city limits was required by law to slow to a crawl. It didn't get too cold in winter, although every few years we saw snow. Summers were hot. By midday, the town could be blistering and your skin would be as sticky as a baby's. But Rock Hill was green, and you could drive past shops on Main Street, then fields of cows and corn—all within minutes. There were streets shaded by tufts of trees. There were stone birdbaths, wisteria, churches, graveyards, a few stoplights, two drive-in "picture shows," hundred-year-old cottages, unpainted rental houses, hand-painted signs, gravel driveways, bikes lying on their sides on front lawns. A down-home rhythm, firmly in place.

Rock Hill's economy was good, healthy, and very much dependent on the Rock Hill Printing and Finishing Company—The Bleachery, as it was called. Built in 1925 on twenty-three acres of land, the mill was owned by M. Lowenstein and Sons, a company based in New York City. The Bleachery grew to be one the largest textile plants in the country. Twenty percent of the people in Rock Hill worked there, bleaching, dying, printing, and finishing cloth, including American and Confederate flags.

In 1956, the workers at The Bleachery went on strike, which meant that Rock Hill's economy faltered and the town did not feel down-home. We wouldn't drive anywhere near those massive brick buildings between White Street and the railroad tracks. So much violence! The people who reported for work ("scabs") were not actually employees but hired just to keep the mill running, so when they tried to cross the picket line to enter the building, the striking workers beat them back with billy clubs and baseball bats. The scabs attacked the strikers, too. Broken bodies on both sides.

The strike went on for almost four months and grew more and more brutal. It wore the edges off everything and everyone. Even away from the mill, right on Main Street, you saw men throwing punches, busting lips. If someone even uttered the words *union* or *labor organizer,* chaos broke out. In the middle of the barbershop, a man jumped on top of another man and pinned him, the poor man flat on his back on the linoleum. There were raw-edged brawls on the front porch of the well-mannered Andrew Jackson Hotel.

It's all anyone could talk about.

Anyone but Mattie. While she freely joined in our dinner conversations as she made her way around the table serving the meal, she also knew when not to join in. She stayed silent if talk touched on race or class. But then, if Mattie were within earshot, we would never introduce such sensitive topics. That would have felt rude. Could cast a pall over everything. Really, though, whom were we protecting? Mattie? Ourselves?

---

My father placed an ad in the *Evening Herald* reassuring striking workers who owed money on their charge accounts at The Smart Shop that if they didn't know when they'd be able to pay, they shouldn't worry. They could take as long as they needed. He was behind them 100 percent.

The morning after the ad ran, two men from New York paid him a visit in the store.

"Stop the ad," they said.

My father's reply: "Why don't you go on back to New York and figure out how to pay your people fair wages? I'll take care of The Smart Shop."

Mother told this story many times over the years. My father would wave it off. "C'mon, Peggy," he'd say. "It was the right thing to do." This was our father, teaching us something, his words modest but radiant with conviction. I loved when Mother told the story. I believe Donald and Brenda loved it, too. We turned the two men from New York who threatened our father into thugs, imitated the way they probably sounded, making our voices deep and gangstery. We'd been rewarded with a father who knew things we only had glimmers of, whose actions perfectly matched his beliefs. Maybe you wouldn't look to him for out-and-out affection. But he never wavered from "doing the right thing." Moral rightness. That's what he was all about.

# 22

Twice a year, my father took the train to New York City to buy the next season's clothing lines for the store. Sometimes, traveling salesmen from New York brought their samples to Rock Hill. When Brenda and I were lucky enough to climb the stairs to our father's office over The Smart Shop and sit in, we were fascinated by the high-pressure salesmen, the racks of clothes they brought, our father in a role so different from how we saw him day-to-day.

Later, in our backyard playhouse, I would play the salesman, holding up a blouse or skirt I'd brought down from my closet, my accent very New York: "This is hot, Bennie! Really hot! You gotta' get this one! It'll fly off the rack!" Brenda played Daddy, her southern accent acquiring an edge, the way his did when he was being a tough sell: "You're crazy! My customers will never go for that!" Back and forth we'd jostle, laughing so hard we had to hold our sides.

One day, in the mid-1950s, my father brought one of those salesmen home for lunch. Mattie was making her way around the breakfast room serving fried chicken, potato salad, slaw, deviled eggs, sliced tomatoes, and biscuits—her standard summer lunch for company. My father, who'd had jury duty the week before, was telling about the murder trial he'd been involved in—the Black man charged, the guilty verdict.

"I don't know," he said, shaking his head wearily, "I'm afraid the other jurors might have let prejudice influence them."

Mattie piped in, "Who was it on trial, Mr. Bennie?"

"Willie Lee Stevenson," my father said.

Mattie had finished taking the oval platter of potato salad around the table and was heading back toward the kitchen. These exact words over her shoulder: "Lord, Mr. Bennie, Willie Lee's the biggest crook on Boyd Hill. He see somethin' he wants—come dark, he gets it. Don't matter what he has to do to get it."

I do not remember anyone's reaction to what Mattie said. It was unusual for my father to mention race in Mattie's presence. And just as unusual for her to chime in. But the most unusual part: My father, so accustomed to *teaching* lessons, seemed to be *learning* a lesson. I believe Mattie was showing him that our judgment is subject to all sorts of biases. That doing the right thing is not always knowable, however broad-minded we aim to be.

# 23

I don't know how many maids my parents had before they hired Mattie, and I don't know where Mattie worked before she came to live with us. I do know that, over the years, my parents hired various part-time maids to work along with Mattie. These women helped with the cleaning and laundry, which meant Mattie could devote more time to cooking and taking care of Donald, Brenda, and me.

Mattie's small, chatty, younger sister, Ethel, worked for us at different times. Equally small, but silent Emma Lee, Mattie's older sister, also worked for us. Mattie's other older sister, Annie Mae, tall, quiet like Emma Lee, sometimes pitched in. Another woman named Ethel, no relation to Mattie, worked part-time for us when I was in junior high school. I remember being surprised that she smoked; I'd never seen a Black woman smoke, certainly not in the presence of white people. After I'd taken driver's ed at school, but before I got my license (at fourteen in South Carolina, so that farm children could drive tractors), Ethel took me out driving many times in our turquoise Studebaker. (My uncle owned a Studebaker dealership in Columbia, which is how we ended up with that needle-nosed car.) Ethel was much more patient than my father when I bumped over a curb turning a corner or didn't give a hand signal because it was raining (no automatic signals then). She gently reminded me to swing out a little before I made my turn or signal with my arm, even if it got wet, all the while puffing on her Pall Mall.

Big, rugged Charlie, with the thin moustache, was our yard-man. In addition to mowing the grass and raking leaves, he taught me how to ride a two-wheel bike, running alongside me on the sidewalk, that long stride of his, holding on to the seat of my new red Schwinn, my front wheel dipping right, then left, all the way to the end of the sidewalk at the bottom of Eden Terrace. A large Black man trotting alongside a little white girl on a bike was not considered unusual in those days. He held on, no matter how much speed I picked up. He did not let go until he saw that I could keep that bike straight and steady. "Keep going," he called out, "keep going!" I remember glancing back for a split second, seeing his big hand waving me on.

When Charlie was too old to work, Lawrence took over. Lawrence was slim but muscular. And charming, always a bright smile on his face. He mowed and raked and also did odd jobs around the house—changed light bulbs, rolled up the rugs to wax the hardwood floors, and, after Rock Hill Concrete Company built a swimming pool in our back yard in 1952, he emptied, then swept the pool with his wide broom each week of the summer and scrubbed the bottom and sides with soapy rags. When the concrete was clean, he turned on the hose, draped it over the side, left it overnight to fill the pool. Sometimes Brenda and I sat on the side and watched him scrub, our suntanned legs swinging, both of us thinking that Lawrence rubbing away the mold in our pool was our very own magic show. What were we thinking? We were turning his hard work into a performance! Something to entertain us on a hot day! He would just look up every now and then, smile that amazing smile, and keep on scrubbing.

---

How do I cross-examine the way it was? My privileged childhood, the world I counted on and cherished—so dependent on Mattie, Annie Mae, Emma Lee, both Ethels, Charlie, and Lawrence. In fact, they gave their lives over to my family. Those were the terms of the bargain, which wasn't exactly a bargain, since only one side drew it up. Their work was not like the work white people I knew did. My father could leave the store early to see me compete in a spelling bee or tap dance in a recital. Even the salesladies in his store had flexibility where you'd want flexibility and stability where you'd want stability. The jobs these Black people had were based on the personal needs of employers, and those needs could shift on a whim.

I don't believe I thought anything about having all this hired help; I was settled down in that place, living my very comfortable life. Everyone who worked for us, it seemed to me, was sweet and cheerful and good company. Of course they were. Keeping their jobs was crucial. *Sweet, cheerful, being good company* was part of the job description.

Children have very little awareness of the actual cogs at work inside their world.

What if I fail to emerge from all this self-investigating with grown-up clarity—deeper than what I might have come to as a child? Can we ever tell the whole truth to ourselves? Insights are tenuous, imperfect. It's so hard to go beyond the familiarity we have with our own stories, interrupt what we've known forever.

# 24

If you lived in Rock Hill and were white, here's what you automatically knew:

The first names (never the last names) of the maids who worked for other families. Viola worked for Dr. Bratton, our pediatrician. Bessie and her grown son, Israel, (and also, Susie) worked for Doc and Granny Sims, Kathryne's grandparents. Lilli Belle worked for Betsy's family. Olivia for Martha Marion's. Rose for Freddy's.

You knew which church everyone attended. Most white people I knew went to Oakland Avenue Presbyterian; St. John's Methodist ran a close second. First Presbyterian was also popular, as was Oakland Baptist and the Episcopal Church of Our Saviour. I knew one family who went to St. Anne's Catholic. Just one. One boy and I were the only kids in our grade who went to a synagogue. (I had nothing to do with him.) There were only twelve Jewish families in the whole town.

You knew whose parents drank too much.

You didn't know any adults who did not smoke.

You knew which friend's mother was having an affair with which friend's father.

You knew whose grown daughters had moved to New York City. When they came back to visit, they were like celebrities. And they *looked* like celebrities. Or maybe foreigners. The clothes they wore. The scarves, how they wore them, glamorously draped around their shoulders or knotted at the neck. How sure of themselves they seemed, even if they'd been gone only a month.

You knew George, the elderly blind man who operated the cranky, old, steel elevator in People's Bank, knew which vegetables he grew in his garden because he kept a shoe-box full of them on the little ledge he rested his arthritic knee on. When we rode his elevator, he always gave Mother a tomato, a cucumber, some squash.

You knew at least one person who lived in the Cobb House, Rock Hill's only apartment building. Seven floors. Our skyscraper. It's where a pair of very old sisters, Mum Reid and Miss Julia, lived, two of the many old people in town Mother took things to, like Mattie's squash casserole or a Christmas poinsettia. Mother also took things to ancient Salome Landauer and her mean husband, Joe, who lived in a house that smelled like mothballs. Brenda and I had never heard of anybody named Salome, so we secretly called her "Salami."

You knew every person at every table in the Elk's Club dining room, where, Saturday evening, your family went for steaks. You also knew the two waitresses, one tall and thin and old, one short and plump and young. You did not know where in the Elk's Club the poker games took place.

You knew Baron Novak, Rock Hill's midget. You did not know how careless and insensitive you were being with the words you used. But Baron joined forces with us—maybe he had no choice but to join forces: He was manager of the football team and wore a jersey with the number ½ printed across the front. You not only knew Baron; you knew the boy who carried his tray down the food line in the lunchroom.

You knew every story of the past and never got sick of hearing them. You knew things would stay just the way they were, never shift, the orderly tune of a town you could count on. All you would ever need.

You didn't know how much you didn't know.

# 25

Certain memories are penetrated with elements of Mattie, even when they have nothing to do with her. This memory is all about my father. But Mattie has always been the lens through which I view race, so even though my father is the key player, I feel the presence of Mattie, on a cellular level, in every detail.

———✳———

Around 1952, my father hired Thelma to work as a maid in The Smart Shop. Thelma was straight-backed, self-possessed, wore lipstick and rouge—unusual for a southern Black woman then. Her hair was styled, I'm sure, in a beauty parlor. More important, she was personable and dynamic—too personable and dynamic not to wait on customers. So, months after hiring her, my father promoted her to saleslady.

But because she was Black, when she wasn't selling, she was still expected to vacuum, mop, dust, clean the toilet and sink in the bathroom, assemble cardboard boxes, unpack and iron new merchandise. The other salesladies in the store were . . . just salesladies. No vacuuming, mopping, dusting, cleaning, assembling, unpacking, or ironing for them.

Customers of The Smart Shop were, of course, white. In Rock Hill in the 1950s, shops catering to white women hired only white salespeople. I imagine, before customers in The Smart Shop fully comprehended that a Black person was waiting on them, before they could raise their eyebrows in disbelief, they'd already found Thelma endearing, so much so that her skin color didn't matter.

Black women shopped down near the railroad tracks, on Trade Street, where the shops included OK Pawn Shop, Jackson's Lunch, Mutt's Pool Hall, Watkin's Hot Dog Stand, and I don't know what else because I was not allowed to set foot on Trade Street. Nobody I knew, none of my friends, ever ventured all the way down Main Street past Friedheim's Department Store, as though, beyond the boundary of the great stone pillars guarding the grand front doors of Rock Hill's oldest department store, it might not be safe for white children. Our territory was well defined.

The one exception—a business that attracted Black and white, rich and poor—was Watkin's Hot Dogs. But it was easy for my mother to pull up to the curb right in front, somebody jump out, run in, order all the hot dogs we could eat for lunch, hop back into the car with those greasy, oniony paper bags, and everything was fine. All I knew about Trade Street was what I happened to glimpse from the back seat of our two-toned green Oldsmobile.

But I was curious. Because what I saw through the window was a carnival-like atmosphere. People on Trade Street seemed to know each other; they shouted back and forth. Clothes hung in the doorway of the pawn shop—outside!—brightly colored dresses and men's shirts, as though the clothes themselves were saying, "Come on in!" Men spilled out of the pool hall laughing and hanging on to each other like great pals, slapping each other on the back. Grown men! In the middle of the afternoon! Not at work! What I saw, or what I thought I saw, was an anything-goes atmosphere, the hours of the day not determining what people should be doing.

I did not believe this was Mattie's street. Mattie, fitting in here? Walking past these stores, with these people, the strap of her big, black handbag tight over her wrist? I could not picture it.

And definitely not farther down Trade Street, away from the bustle, where I saw, mid-mornings, a cluster of Black men standing on the corner. They were silent, hardly moving, as if they were suspended there. An old truck would pull up, and you could hear the white driver call out through his open window, "I need two!"

or "I need five!" Whatever number he named, that's how many Black men climbed up into the truck bed. With a rattle, off they'd go. Then another truck would pull up, another driver's bidding, another climb into the truck. When there were no more trucks, the few men left standing on the sidewalk ambled off. It was years before I understood this was how some businesses in Rock Hill got day workers.

But here's the main thing: On Main Street, Thelma was, by many years, the first Black salesperson. And that was a significant risk for Thelma. A significant risk for my father. In 1952. Deep South. Small town. Everyone knew everything that was going on. And some people didn't mind throwing their opinions around.

There was only one bathroom in The Smart Shop. A room barely big enough for a toilet and sink. A room with a creaky, narrow-planked, wood floor you'd get splinters from if you walked across it barefoot. The room had a window, but it was so tiny and scarred and high up on the wall, daylight barely entered. The light switch was iffy; you had to hit it twice.

This bathroom was in the back of the store, just before you got to the rear door, which opened to the sooty alleyway where my father parked his car on a steep slant every morning. The bathroom was so small. Insignificant, really. Not anything you would ever think could cause a problem.

# 26

Days after Thelma had been promoted to saleslady, Brenda and I were asleep in our beds. I was eleven; she was fourteen. Donald was nineteen and away at college. Our parents were downstairs in our knotty-pine den, watching television, late for them to still be up, but TV was a novelty, since our set—a radio, TV, and stereo combo in a wormy-chestnut console—was new. Mattie was in her room, door closed. She was either reading her Bible or asleep.

The doorbell rang. The sound bore through every room in the house. Bore through my stomach. Who could be ringing the bell at this hour?

Brenda threw off her covers and slid her feet into her furry slippers. She padded quickly out to the landing. I was used to following her, so I just as quickly threw off my covers and slid into my slippers. By the time I made it down the two steps to the landing, she was already stretched out on her stomach, that long, thin body, tall for her age. How did she know this was where we needed to be? But she always knew. I noticed, in the seconds before she'd left our room, she'd managed to grab her glasses from her bedside table. (I loved those glasses. Soon after she'd gotten them in the fifth grade, she decided she didn't like the clear plastic frame, so she painted it with red nail polish.) I lay down beside her, the scratchy wall-to-wall carpet biting my legs. I shifted my skinny little body to get comfortable. Brenda wrapped her fingers around the railing and peered through. I did the same.

Right away, I saw Mr. Blankenship, the husband of Opal Blankenship, a saleslady in The Smart Shop. I knew his puffy shape, his too-full face. He had taken a step over the threshold and was standing on the round hooked rug in our entrance hall. I could see a reflection of his body in profile in the floor-to-ceiling antique pier mirror off to the side. He appeared wobbly, weaving just a little, side to side. Was he drunk? He was a mess—straggly black hair not combed, tie pulled loose, overcoat hanging crooked. He looked like a *Saturday Evening Post* cartoon of a man who'd had one too many. In the cartoon, the man would have stars for eyeballs.

My father was standing across from Mr. Blankenship. He was wearing his beige wool robe. I could see his navy-and-white-striped cotton pajama legs. His long, skinny, size 12 brown leather slippers were fixed solid in one spot.

I huddled closer to Brenda, curved a little into her.

Mother was wearing her pink quilted flannel robe and stood behind my father, a little to the side so that she was hidden slightly by him but still had a clear view of Mr. Blankenship. It looked like she was wringing her hands, although maybe I just imagined her wringing her hands. She was a hand-wringer. A worrier. Maybe I imagined her wringing her hands because I felt like wringing *my* hands. I couldn't see her face so I had no idea what her expression was. But I imagined a fretful look.

Suddenly, like a swell of thunder, Mr. Blankenship bellowed right in my father's face: *"The ladies don't want no nigger using the goddamned bathroom!"*

I felt like I'd been punched in the chest. Like the whole house got punched in the chest. My first thought: Did Mattie hear? No, no, Mattie, please be asleep. Be fast asleep. I could not bear her being punched in the chest. I glanced over my shoulder at the door to her room. Still shut. Good. Let her door be like a concrete slab. No sound passing through. She didn't hear. She didn't hear. I had to believe that.

———∞∞———

Earlier the same evening, after dinner, in the den, away from Mattie's ears—she was doing the dishes—my father had told Mother, Brenda, and me about a meeting he'd called in the store late that afternoon, just before everyone left for home. He'd gathered the salesladies—everyone but Thelma—in the little area near the back, where the winter coats hung, where a sign my father had hand-painted framed the top of the doorway leading to the rear of the store: *Whether your purchase is large or small, or none at all, you are always welcome at The Smart Shop.*

What he said to them went something like this: "I've been hearing some talk among you ladies about Thelma using the bathroom. Here's the situation: We have one bathroom. And everyone who works here is welcome to use it. If you don't like this arrangement, you can leave right now."

———∞∞———

My father's reaction to Mr. Blankenship that night? He stood up straighter, more businesslike, a posture we all were familiar with. I could see his clean, strong jaw. Then he took a step *toward* Mr. Blankenship, not away. Everyone who knew Ben Kurtz knew he was fearless. Knew how deeply principled he was.

I'm sure he must have spoken to Mr. Blankenship. And I'm sure his voice was measured, not angry. Not meek either. Just firm. I was so nervous for him, though, that his words are totally lost to me now. It might have been that he didn't say anything at that point. Is this possible? After Mr. Blankenship's words exploded and blew up our entire entrance hall, cracked the pier mirror down the middle, shook the hanging brass light fixture, jiggled the pointy crystals dangling from the chandelier in the dining room, made the flowers in the wallpaper in the tiny guest bathroom at the back of the house drop their leaves, is it possible my father did not say a word?

My head was narrow enough to poke almost through the railing. I wasn't worried about getting stuck, although I almost did. Brenda pulled me back, one sure finger hooked inside the neck of my pajamas. That's the thing about my sister: I might not have been her favorite person, but she would never let harm come to me. Once, she beat up the neighborhood bully because he'd thrown a rock at me. Pernettia was out hanging clothes and heard the bully screaming and crying. She had to pull Brenda off him.

Even after Brenda yanked me back from the railing, I could still see the scene unfolding below. Our father was gently easing Mr. Blankenship out the front door, down the front steps. I'm sure of this part: Neither of them was saying a word now. It was so quiet and the door had been flung open so wide, I could hear Mr. Blankenship's car noisily idling in the driveway, probably blowing dirty puffs of exhaust into the wintry air.

I imagined our father and Mr. Blankenship stepping off the bottom step onto our front concrete patio, circling the white metal chairs and tables, the two of them doing some kind of spooky dance, the air between them charged. They would then cross the stepping stones to our gravel driveway and Mr. Blankenship's car. I imagined the stars in the sky snapping on and off.

Mother had moved into the doorway, but stayed inside the house. I could see her leaning forward, watching, tying and untying the sash on her robe.

Then I heard my father's voice, steady, unyielding, gentle really, but anyone who knew him would know he meant business. I can hear his words even now, this many years later. I will never forget them: "I've already said everything I'm going to say on this subject. I think you better go on home now."

# 27

To someone who didn't know better, it sounded like my father had a South Carolina accent, the slow cadence and plush vowels. He was born in Opelika, Alabama, but spent his growing-up years in La-Grange, Georgia, and his was definitely a Georgia accent. If you grew up in the South, you could usually tell where somebody was from.

My father attended Auburn University for one year, but for his sophomore year, when family funds grew scarce, he transferred to Newberry College in Newberry, South Carolina, a town where a family friend, Harry Vigodsky, gave him a part-time job in his shoe store. Brenda and I knew this story well: It had been hard to find work then; the Depression was approaching; this was the only job available to our father. He was seventeen (he'd entered college at sixteen). Brenda's and my favorite part of the story? We could make each other snort with laughter just by uttering the name, Vigodsky. We were only two generations away from grandparents who'd emigrated to this country from Eastern Europe and Russia. Yet my sister and I were so southern, so ensconced in the Gentile world of Rock Hill, we could laugh ourselves silly at the exotic syllables of a Russian Jewish immigrant's name.

Our father graduated from Newberry College in 1929, then moved to Atlanta to attend Emory Law School. After his second year, his father died and our father had to drop out of law school to find full-time work to support his mother, his two older brothers, two older sisters, and twin sister. No one in his family thought it was odd that the youngest child took responsibility for his mother and five siblings. This is when he moved back to Newberry and began working full-time in Harry Vigodsky's shoe store.

Mother was born in Denmark, South Carolina, lived most of her childhood and young adulthood there, although her family moved a good bit, from town to town in the Carolinas. Her father, a department store owner, was not only a poor businessman; he gambled. He won big, and he lost big. Sometimes the family had to move in the middle of the night. Mother attended the University of South Carolina, studying to be a CPA—the only female in the accounting school. But in her junior year, she had to drop out because her father had declared bankruptcy yet again. She moved back to Denmark and worked as a bookkeeper for South Carolina Power and Light. She met my father at a dance in Columbia. They were married in 1932, settled in Newberry, then moved to Rock Hill in 1934. That's the year my father opened The Smart Shop.

A little over a decade later, his mother, Grandma Kurtz, pale and on her deathbed, eased out of a coma to make him promise he'd take care of his brothers and sisters.

My father followed his mother's directive. He opened a men's clothing store in Rock Hill for one of his brothers to run; everyone thought my uncle owned King's Men's Shop, a couple of blocks down Main Street from The Smart Shop, and that misbelief was fine with my father. He partnered with another brother in a store in Concord, North Carolina; partnered with a cousin in a store in Salisbury, North Carolina. When he took over the women's floor in a department store in Columbia, he hired his older sister, who was divorced and needed income, to be his manager. He didn't just hand over the keys to these different relatives; he stayed involved, guiding and advising. He guided and advised some relatives more than others (particularly my Uncle Easy, who, in my father's opinion, was *too* easygoing). Guiding and advising might not be the words his siblings would have used. But for my father, it always came down to this: doing things the right way.

# 28

The night after Mr. Blankenship's visit, my father arrived home from work, hung his overcoat and felt hat on the wooden coat rack in the front hall, and signaled with a nod for Mother to rise from the loveseat in the den to follow him into the back hall.

Brenda and I were sprawled on our stomachs across the rug in the den, playing cards, our hair falling around our faces. She was probably winning. If I'd been winning, we would not still be playing. Our father's gesture was surprising. He usually didn't speak to any of us, did not acknowledge us in any way, when he first came home in the evening. The rule in our house was, after all those long hours at work, he needed peace and quiet, time to read the *Evening Herald* on the leather sofa in the den, under the gold light from the floor lamp. From what I could tell, this was pretty much the rule in my friends' houses as well. The explanation in *our* family—articulated by Mother more than once—was that he had to listen to female voices in the store all day, so the females in our house needed to just be silent when he came home. We never questioned the reasonableness of such a rule. It's just the way it was.

I could barely make out my father's hushed words to Mother in the back hall, but they went something like this: "The talk on Main Street was that Mr. Blankenship was so enraged he brought a loaded gun when he came to the house last night."

*A gun! In Mr. Blankenship's coat pocket! In our front hall! The three of them—my father, my mother, Mr. Blankenship. And a gun. All this to keep Thelma from sitting down on the same toilet as Mrs. Blankenship.*

I couldn't hear Mother's answer, if she did answer. I imagine her whispering, *A gun, a gun,* over and over. I couldn't see her face, or my father's face, as he reported this horrifying news. I couldn't see the mahogany telephone table, which they were standing beside. Or the Rock Hill phone book that was so thin it was practically a pamphlet on its shelf beneath the seat connected to the table, this small town we lived in, so small we thought we knew its people. I could only feel fear spiraling deep in my rib cage, the weight of it all, how hatreds can rise up and then there is really nothing, nothing at all, we can do to keep everyone safe.

# 29

Years passed. Times were changing. Hems got shorter, dresses more colorful. My father closed the millinery department, stopped selling white gloves, started selling white boots. It was the early 1960s.

My father promoted Thelma again to full-time saleslady. No more maid duties. Thelma was so good at what she did, many customers—still, all white—now requested her. My father would probably have said she was one of the top three salesladies, along with the two powdered older women who'd worked at The Smart Shop since the day it opened back in 1934. These two women were Miss Cauthen and Miss Smith, although they were called "Cauthen" and "Smith." When I was little, I could not tell them apart. They were both pudgy, plain, and wore drapey black dresses and little wire-rimmed glasses that slipped down their noses.

Mrs. Blankenship still worked for my father. But she was not among the top three. She was loud, brash, talked too much, not one of my father's favorite employees. Someone like that would never be my father's favorite anything.

Black people were being hired all over town, but only in stores that served both Black and white customers, like the hardware store and drug store, and only in stores in which merchandise was not so personal. Stores that did not sell dresses and blouses and skirts and slips.

Thelma was still the only Black salesperson in a clothing store on Main Street.

And she was the only employee of The Smart Shop who was called by her first name.

The complicated ethics of my father. Of course, he would promote a Black woman to sales. She deserved it. It didn't matter whether other shop owners were doing this or not. Didn't matter whether anyone approved. Or objected. But Black women did not shop in The Smart Shop. Was it simply a matter of economics, the prices at The Smart Shop out of reach for most Black women in Rock Hill? Was it that white women at that time and in that place would not want to try on dresses, blouses, skirts, and slips that had been tried on by Black women? Or was it another example of just about everyone—Black and white—knowing and accepting where society said they belonged? Even my father, ethical as he was, did not push against that.

# 30

Fifty years later, in 2015, my parents dead for over thirty-five years, Brenda dead for close to ten, I was scrolling through "Memories of Growing Up in Rock Hill" on Facebook and came across an article from the *Evening Herald* published in the early 1960s.

The headline: *Furniture Salesman and Maid in Ladies Clothing Store Win Acclaim as Rock Hill's Friendliest Employes* [sic].

Thelma! Voted Rock Hill's friendliest female employee!

But.

Maid?

Why did they call her a maid, when she was a salesperson? If she were a maid, nobody would have encountered her in the store, so nobody would know to vote for her. Maybe it was risky in the early 1960s, even reckless, to broadcast her sales status. Were the editors protecting her? Or were they protecting themselves? After all, what small-town southern newspaper would want to rile its customer base? Or did the editors automatically call a Black female worker a maid, regardless of the job she was paid for? Or was it the voting customers who assumed, because of the color of her skin, that she was a maid—even though, every day, all day, she was right there in the front of the store, greeting customers by name, admiring them as they admired themselves in the three-way mirrors, ringing up their purchases? Was it my father who, growing more cautious with age, backed down? Was he avoiding placing Thelma in harm's way? Avoiding placing himself in harm's way?

How I want to plop down beside him on the sofa—after giving him time to relax and catch his breath after a long day in the store, all those women talking, high-pitched voices, chatter, chatter. My father would let the newspaper drift down to his lap. He'd turn toward me, light a Lucky Strike, take a puff, the smell of smoke silky and gritty, both at the same time. He'd smile his tired, lopsided smile, drape one arm around my shoulder or touch my hand. Finally, the intimate link I'd always wanted with this honest, brave, fair man. I would shyly point out how they'd called Thelma a maid in the newspaper, be quick to say (regardless of whose idea it was to use the word) that I realize the climb to high moral ground often ends up with us falling back or wandering off, our attention once again on our narrow little lives.

But who, Daddy, after all those sales she rang up—I can just hear the brass cash register dinging—who called Thelma a maid? And why?

# 31

Mother was sunny, vivacious, so alive she practically pulsed. She was optimistic and trusted in the goodness of others. She was completely *with* you. She was completely with everyone she knew or ever met.

One late afternoon in the 1950s, she was at my father's desk upstairs in The Smart Shop, working on the books. My father was downstairs, greeting customers, overseeing everything. She decided to take a break, slip next door to Good Drug Store for a Coke. She believed everybody should have a Coke around four or five o'clock, "to hold you over." As though Coke were a health food.

This particular late-afternoon break, Mother was gone longer than usual. My father decided to check on her, make sure everything was all right. There, in the back of Good Drugs, near the pharmacy, squeezed into a booth for four, my father saw six people: Mother and a Native American family—a man and woman and their three young children. As my father got closer, he saw that the man was drawing a map on a paper napkin—*you go down this road, then you turn left, go seven miles, then you look for* . . . Mother was listening hard, studying the inky map. The man was giving Mother directions to his house on the Catawba Reservation, ten miles outside of Rock Hill. Mother had started a conversation with them, maybe paid some attention to the children, joined them in the booth, and now she would visit the family the following Sunday afternoon. She ended up staying in touch with them for years.

In the 1950s, for a white person in Rock Hill to know a Catawba Indian, to visit in his home on the reservation—I did not know anyone but my mother who did this. The only whites who ever visited the reservation were children taken in school buses to see the clay pottery the Catawba Indians had been molding by hand since the Revolutionary War. Most people in Rock Hill knew Chief Blue's name. And knew what he looked like. For a quarter, you could have your picture taken with him Saturday mornings in front of the newsstand on Main Street. His feathered headdress, fringed buckskin shirt, beaded moccasins, the woven blanket draped over one shoulder. The smile Chief Blue flashed for every single photo.

---

It's not until I've written about my mother and her deeds, my father and his, that I finally understand that these stories explain Mattie and our family.

When I began writing this book and was just getting my parents' stories down on paper, I kept questioning myself: *I'm writing a book about Mattie; yet there are all these pages about my mother and father. Do they even belong here? Why do I keep trying to wedge them in?*

In the prologue, I'd written: "Like thousands of white southerners in my generation, I was raised by a Black woman. . . ." For sure, there were many others in my social class, at that time, who were like me. But what was radically different was Mattie's place in our family. She was the maid, yes. She cooked, cleaned, took care of the children, particularly the youngest, me. And she was paid for this work. But she was part of our family. Not part of our family the way other maids were part of the families they worked for. Not *peripherally* part of our family. *Truly* part of our family. And she remained truly part of our family until the day she died.

I remember a friend of Mother's being surprised, before my parents added on their master bedroom and bath, that the six of us used the tiny bathroom at the top of the stairs—my parents, Mattie, my brother, sister, and me. (Again, a problem bathroom!) The woman wasn't questioning how one bathroom could be enough for six people. That situation would not be so unusual. "You mean

Mattie uses the same bathroom"—her eyes wide with disbelief—"as all y'all?" I'd never even thought about it. Why wouldn't we all use the same bathroom? Isn't that what a family does? And we would celebrate Christmas together. It's what a family does. And we'd celebrate each other's birthdays in a grand, expansive way.

But I did not know another family who lived this way.

The question becomes, *why* did we live this way?

I've had people close to us attribute my parents' open-mindedness to their being Jewish. *Of course, Jews are tolerant of minorities. They're minorities themselves.*

But that's not it.

We lived this way because of who my mother and father were. The qualities they possessed created our world. My father's sense of right and wrong. Mother's empathy. What was true for both of them: If someone lives in your house, they're family.

What was true for my parents within the walls of our house was also true for them outside those walls—when my father promoted Thelma to the position she deserved in The Smart Shop, when my father looked out for his customers during the Bleachery strike, when my father tried to talk the rest of the jury into declaring a Black man innocent, when Mother admonished people cutting in line ahead of Mattie at the bus station, when she visited a family on the Catawba Reservation, the same way she'd visit any family in their home.

In that place, in that time, these were big gestures. My parents were bridging gaps nobody I knew was bridging. At the same time, you wouldn't exactly say they were on a mission. There were many people, even back then, who were doing the really hard work of trying to right wrongs. You could say that what my parents did, from a broader perspective, was actually quite small.

Still, they set a lasting example for our family. Again and again, they showed us what was important to them: Fairness (our father). Connection (our mother). When you think about it, that's pretty big.

# 32

I don't remember when I finally met Mattie's daughter, don't remember the minute Minnie and I found ourselves face-to-face for the first time, when she was no longer just a detail of Mattie's life, but now part of mine. It was when she was a teenager, I believe, maybe in high school, and I was around five or six. Maybe she came to visit Mattie at our house on Eden Terrace. Yes. That had to be it. I don't believe we would have gone to visit her.

Once Minnie and I entered each other's lives, the distance between us felt thin to me. Our connection was, of course, Mattie. I know that when I say this, I sound as though I believe I had as strong a claim on Mattie as Minnie did. I did not. Money bought what I had. Minnie had what money could not buy—Mattie had brought her into the world. They shared blood. But oh, what Minnie did not have. All at the expense of what I had.

It was easy to like Minnie. She was warm and friendly to everyone in my family. Almost floral in her beauty and grace. I mean she was pretty without any makeup. Her smile was confident, her eyes long-lashed. Her skin was lighter than Mattie's, and smooth. She wore her hair long and loose, almost springy, unusual for a Black girl then.

When she was a student at historically Black Johnson C. Smith University in Charlotte in the 1950s, she was voted the school's beauty queen, which meant she would ride on the back of an open convertible in Rock Hill's Christmas parade. Rock Hill did not have enough beauty queens, so we imported a few from neighboring towns.

The day of the parade, it was frigid, blustery, maybe a little icy, maybe just wintry cold. Our family—my parents, Donald (home from college for the holidays), Brenda, Mattie, and I—watched from our overheated spot upstairs over The Smart Shop, racks of layaways around us, flattened cardboard boxes ready to be assembled, our father's dusty wood desk, his papers, ledger, black telephone. The six of us, along with the salesladies who worked in the store, huddled around the wide, streaked windows looking out over Main Street.

Marching bands from white high schools led off the parade. Then, the band from Emmett Scott, the only Black public high school in town. This band won more prizes, was better known, than any band in the Carolinas. The drum major out front was the star of every parade, his tall plumed hat, long legs, the way he twirled his baton, flinging it high in the air, grabbing it mid-spin. He and the majorettes and the band—the drums and brass, their bold throb—filled the street from sidewalk to sidewalk.

Which then led to the floats: The Shriners float and Uncle Morris playing the organ. A Founders' Day float, on which men and women were dressed like pioneers, doing pioneer things, like churning butter. The Bleachery float. The Rock Hill National Bank float—a girl from my school got to ride on that, since her father was president of the bank.

Next, the fire trucks.

And finally, the beauty queens on the backs of convertibles, one slowly following another. Miss Rock Hill. Miss Civil Defense. Miss Rock Hill High School. Miss Winthrop Training School. Miss Fort Mill. The Carousel Queen from Charlotte. Miss Emmett Scott. And, just before the fake-snowy float carrying Santa Claus, which always marked the end of the parade: the beauty queen we'd been waiting to see, Miss Johnson C. Smith.

"There she is!" one of us probably cried out. If we pressed ourselves to the windows and looked all the way to the right, we could see the Ford convertible carrying Minnie turning onto Main Street, up near the Andrew Jackson Hotel. She was sitting high on the shoulder of the back seat, wearing a strapless gown, long white gloves, and a tiara that glistened against the gray-white sky. The way she was dressed, you'd think it was a toasty June afternoon. I loved what she wore, the gown, the gloves, how she waved and turned her perfect face from left to right, giving the crowds of people on both sides of the street a chance to see her. We watched her car roll slowly along, now beneath our window, then down Main Street, all the way to the train station, where Trade Street crossed Main Street. The parade always turned right onto Trade Street and continued on from there, I'm not sure where. I thought her appearance on Main Street was just a brief stopover on her way to Hollywood.

I remember the six of us in the car driving home, my father behind the wheel, Mother beside him, smoking, her graceful hand flicking the ashes into the tiny ashtray beneath the radio dial, Mattie and Donald and Brenda and me in the back seat, curled in close, our wool coats heavy, hands shoved deep in our pockets until the heat in the car kicked in. What was Mattie thinking? Did she wish we were going to find Minnie to congratulate her, maybe invite her to the house to celebrate? Did we talk about Minnie at all? Did my parents, Donald, Brenda, or I wonder about Minnie's life, was she living in a dorm, what was she majoring in, what would she do when she graduated, how she and Donald were so close in age, one headed home with Mattie, one not?

# 33

I declared myself a poet when I was in the third grade. Then I took a break from poetry until junior high, when I heaved myself into adolescence and boys began breaking my heart. Poem after poem, lovesick little things. Then I took another break, a long one. I didn't write again until I was in my late thirties. That's when I began taking my writing seriously, signing up for poetry workshops, studying the work of established poets; every spare minute, writing, writing. I still have a copy of the first poem I wrote as an adult, pecked out on Mother's old, green, portable Olivetti, now mine—the uneasy fretwork of my words:

> *Your Baby*
>
> *You spread love through my childhood*
> *like honey, your face*
> *cool, smooth and Hershey brown*
> *against my pale pink cheek. Your hands*
> *smelled like the peaches you sliced*
> *and served in cream. Sweet gospel hymns,*
> *your sweet gospel hymns, Jesused through*
> *slow August nights.*
>
> *I wonder, Mattie, while you pressed*
> *the eyelet of my blouses into stiffened butterflies,*

*parted my hair and brushed loose the tangles,*
*while you called me your baby,*
*who did all this for your Minnie?*

The poem is not good. My reference to love—using the actual *word,* love—is pretty sentimental. And then, there's all that stored-up white guilt. Not exactly subtle. And why do we white people insist on comparing the color of a Black person's skin to food? Also, those too-cute eyelet blouses. I never published the poem. For good reason. Never even showed it to anyone. I held on to it for years, wanting to write about Mattie and Minnie and me—my mind looping around and around the subject—but I knew what a risk it was. Too easy to exaggerate Mattie's and my relationship, to get into apologizing for the way things were. And how to stay true to Mattie's and Minnie's history—their individual histories and their shared history—when, at that point, I knew so little of either?

I wrote the poem, restraint took over, I put the poem away.

# 34

Minnie left Johnson C. Smith University before graduating, married, moved to New York City with her husband, gave birth to three daughters, divorced pretty soon after her third daughter was born, returned to college, graduated when her oldest was thirteen, taught kindergarten. While she was raising her daughters alone and teaching, she earned a master's degree. Two of her daughters eventually moved to California, one remained in New York City. They married, had children of their own, and all three earned master's degrees and taught school.

During the two years (1965 to 1967) I lived and worked in New York City after college, I took the subway twice from my apartment on East 70th Street to Harlem: once, soon after I'd moved there, to visit Minnie; once, to see Mattie, when she'd taken the train up to spend a few days with Minnie.

In 1988, Brenda and I were both married, with children, living blocks from each other in Charlotte. We decided to have a seventieth birthday luncheon for Mattie at Brenda's house. Minnie, newly retired from teaching but substitute-teaching, rode the bus down for the party. (Like Mattie, she did not like to fly.) I picked her and Mattie up in Rock Hill, swung by for Pernettia and Mckie, Mattie's friend who was called by her last name, and the five of us, in my boxy Volvo, were happily off to the celebration. Three other friends of Mattie's, all from Rock Hill, rode with Ethel, Mattie's sister, who had worked for Brenda in recent years and knew the way.

We started off with champagne and Brenda's appetizers—her onion mixture on little rye toasts, her shrimp mousse and crackers —and then we found our place cards around the table. Big platters of my chicken salad, pasta salad, green salad, and Brenda's home-made sourdough bread were on the table. Later, Brenda's chocolate sheet cake.

When I was little, Mattie called me her baby. Or, child. In later years, she called Brenda and me her "white children." She would introduce us to any neighbor or church friend who happened to stop by her house when we were there: "These are my white chil-dren!" At the birthday luncheon, Mattie's white children had the honored seats. Mattie's Black child was one chair over. Mattie sat between Brenda and me, Minnie on the other side of me. The excitement of the day, mixed with Mattie's happiness and pride, the energy of our guests—all that was rising in me, and I don't re-member even being concerned about how we were arranged around the table. Maybe Brenda decided where the place cards would go. I'm sure she made the place cards; she was the artist in the family. I could've weighed in. But didn't. Then again, maybe I set out the place cards.

I was glad, though, to be seated next to Minnie. I'd always wanted to have a conversation with her about her childhood. My poem about the triangle Mattie, Minnie, and I formed—one child coming into being with the mother, one without—was actually one big question. I wasn't sure how bringing up this subject with her would work, how she would react, how I would feel about her answers, what I would say in response to her answers, whether we could even talk privately, given our surroundings and how close we all sat around the table.

But at one point during lunch, while conversation swirled around us, I turned to Minnie to say that I wanted to ask her about a few things I'd always been curious about. Looking back on this moment, I wonder if I was conscious of preparing my face in any way as I opened the conversation. I do know that I asked her where she had lived while she was growing up.

She acted as though my question were perfectly reasonable, and she answered in a soft, deliberate way, with the same confidence in her bearing I'd always seen: "I was raised by my aunt and uncle in Charlotte, Mattie's older brother and his wife."

I'd heard Minnie refer to Mattie by her first name, not *Mother,* so hearing her say *Mattie* did not surprise me. I'd also met this aunt and uncle; I'd driven Mattie to their house in the Wilmore neighborhood, not far from the Charlotte airport, several times.

I told Minnie I felt really bad about that. Of course, I explained, I loved Mattie with all my heart, but Minnie should have been the one to live with her, to be raised by her, not me.

Minnie put her hand on mine, both our hands now resting on the table, and she said something like: "Oh no, I had wonderful parents." She used the word *parents*. "I loved them very much. And Mattie would come visit. Pretty often."

We were turned toward each other, our bodies sideways to the table, her hand still holding mine. Her fingernails, neatly filed, clear polish.

And then, with no guardedness, she smiled, looked frankly at me, and said these exact words: "I thought Mattie was my aunt. Just a very loving aunt."

*She'd thought Mattie was her aunt!*

*Did I know that Mattie had a daughter before Minnie knew she was her daughter?*

Minnie said she had *fond memories*—her words—of coming to visit Mattie when Mattie was living with us, how kind my mother had always been to Minnie. She talked about the books Mother gave her when she was a child, the outfits from the store when she was a teenager. I don't remember any of those visits.

And then she said, "Your mama was the sweetest person I've ever known. And you are just like your mama."

She told me she loved coming to our house, how beautiful it was. She remembered our pool. (Did she ever swim in that pool? I didn't ask; she didn't say. I think I know the answer.)

I was wholly absorbed, though, in what she *did* say, watching her lips as she shaped her words. She didn't really look like Mattie, but something about each one's self-assurance made you think she did.

Minnie didn't say when she was told that Mattie was her mother. And I didn't ask. She also didn't say who told her, nor how she felt hearing the news. She did say she understood that Mattie would not have been able to raise her; she would not have been able to work and also take care of a child. She knew that Mattie had dreams for her—a good and secure future. Minnie said she could imagine how difficult Mattie's decision had been—to hand her child over to her brother and sister-in-law. And she said that she had always been grateful for the life my family gave Mattie and, in turn, gave her. She said she knew the advantages she had enjoyed were made possible by Mattie's *connection*—the word she used, instead of *employment*—with our family.

Nowhere in her conversation that day was there any mention of the burdens she had endured as a result of her mother taking care of me instead of her. As though she were placing her own history inside a larger cultural view. As though she were reassuring me that she did not feel any resentment toward my family or me. She said she had always understood that her situation was not unusual in the 1940s and '50s, how Black women went to work in white folks' homes in order to give their own children what they themselves did not have, and Mattie had been fortunate to end up with my family.

Who was I to deny how Minnie interpreted her particular and peculiar situation? Could I have taken in an indictment of my family, had it been forthcoming? While I felt it in my bones that she was being honest with me, not holding back, not blaming my family, did I really have the ability to assess what she was saying? Was I just hearing what I wanted to hear?

And then, the conversation was over. I knew that I should not ask any more questions. Regardless of how straightforward it seemed Minnie had been during that birthday celebration for Mattie, I sensed there were places I wasn't allowed to go, places I would not be allowed to enter.

# 35

In 1954—I was thirteen—my parents decided it was no longer necessary for Mattie to live with us, so my father helped her rent a small white clapboard house across town, on the other side of the railroad tracks. I was excited for Mattie, as though she were going off to college. How proud I was of her, how independent she had suddenly become. Imagine! Mattie ready to live on her own! No awareness on my part that this was a grown woman who'd lived with a family *as part of her job* and was no longer needed in that capacity. Oh, the limits to my awareness, to taking in the lessons my parents were trying to teach me! What is accurate, I believe, is that each of us—Mattie, my parents, my brother and sister and I—understood the enormity of this move. But we were ready for it. We had all grown accustomed to the idea gradually, over a span of months, and it felt right. Mattie and I talked about it. She said that she was sad to leave me, but it would be nice to have her own place. Of course, she'd continue to work for my family; she just wouldn't live with us. I was sad for her to live elsewhere, but I couldn't wait to visit, to see how she decorated her living room, smell the cooking smells in her kitchen.

She lived in that house for a few years, but then one night, while she was visiting Minnie in New York City (train fare was one of Mattie's Christmas gifts), the house burned to the ground. Faulty wiring. My father then hired a contractor to build a larger, three-bedroom, brick house for her, as though brick (good, solid brick) and size (nice and substantial) would fix the house in its spot on Clarinda Street. I think of that second house as my father's way of walking everything back to safety. He paid for the house in full, so that Mattie could live there, mortgage-free, forever. And she did live in that house forever, until long after my parents had died, until she was old and frail, and she—always practical, accepting things as they were—was ready to move into a nursing home.

Mattie's new house was on a newly created street in a small, very nice neighborhood of young Black families and elderly Black people, well-kept yards, basketball hoops in driveways, wheelchair ramps, outdoor grills. It was one street over from a well-to-do white neighborhood, the only Black neighborhood in Rock Hill so close to upscale whites. Ironically, the street that led into Mattie's neighborhood was named Lucky Street.

A woman Mattie's age lived next door. Delsey Mae and Mattie called each other every night before they went to bed to make sure the other was all right. Whenever I visited Mattie—and especially if I brought my children and later, my grandchildren—we always popped in to see Delsey Mae next door. When the two of them were in their eighties, Delsey Mae became too arthritic to live alone, and her children moved her to a nursing home in Columbia. Shortly after, Mattie, at eighty-nine, moved into a nursing home in Rock Hill.

---

When Mattie was still in her early seventies, the neighborhood began changing. The city did not maintain those streets. A public housing project was built a few houses down from her. She felt less safe. She began renting her third bedroom to male students from Friendship Junior College, a two-year, historically Black, Baptist school in Rock Hill. Most of these boarders were athletes—rangy basketball players, husky football players. Mattie called them "my boys." She cooked for them. They looked after her—helped clean the house, took out the garbage, changed light bulbs, mowed the grass. Even after they were grown, "her boys" stayed in touch through letters and phone calls, traveled back to Rock Hill to see her, brought their wives and children to meet her. They all returned to Rock Hill, years later, for her funeral.

When you walked out Mattie's back door, down the three steps, you found yourself up to your knees in her garden—masses and tangles of corn, tomatoes, squash, cucumbers, green peppers, butter beans. She was always planting a new variety of something. The divoted rows stretched from one side of her property to the other. Mattie planted just as large a garden for Delsey Mae. The two end-to-end gardens appeared as long as a football field. Vegetables, earthworms, bees, bugs, butterflies, birds, snakes, all thrived there. How was it that the only gardens in the entire country that got just the right amount of sun, just the right amount of rain, the right afternoon and evening temperatures, were on Clarinda Street? Those last years Mattie was in her house, I can see her in her long, white, cotton nightgown, plucking tomatoes off the leafy vines for me to take home. "Here. Take more, child. You know how good Early Girls are."

In her front yard, grass turned green in the summer and brown in the winter. She said that was the way grass was supposed to be. You don't need all those chemicals if you just plant the right grass seed and you're okay with it looking half-dead in cold weather. Rose bushes, their petaled wonder, lined one side of her yard. A dogwood near the curb bloomed pure white, spring after spring, even after most dogwoods across the South had been stricken with disease. On either side of her front porch: flowers, flowers, flowers, their wild, sweet smells, seedpods blowing, roots crosshatching deep in the soil, carrying coneflowers, black-eyed Susans, Becky daisies, and phlox to new spots everywhere. When I think of her front yard, I picture a child's drawing: grass, flowers, sun.

# 36

It was September 1956, and I would turn fifteen in a month. All my friends were at one of those Sunday night church youth group meetings. I would have been with them—I was a permanent guest who happened to be Jewish—but that night I had a bad cold, so I was moping on the sofa, feeling sorry for myself, tuning in to our one television channel, trusty old WBTV, not imagining that the season premiere of *The Ed Sullivan Show* would introduce Mattie and me to a roiling god who sang like a gate swinging off its rusted hinges.

She and I were side by side on the sofa, the ottoman pulled close so that we could both rest our feet. I'm sure she needed to rest her feet more than I did.

We were the only ones home. My parents were out of town; Brenda was with her friends; Donald was working in Columbia before being drafted into the Army. Mattie was spending the night with me. If I were going to share a big, rare moment of musical clarity with anyone, I'd choose her. Her hymns had hovered over my childhood, led me to rhythm and blues, to Gene Nobles, the disc jockey who played Black singing groups on WLAC radio in Nashville, which I listened to, lights out, volume low, late at night, every night.

Black singers on the radio or TV were rare then. You had to search the dial. I resented The Crew-Cuts and their very white version of "Sh-Boom," which got more air play and became more popular than the one by The Chords, who were Black. Not unusual, though, for a Black group to record a song first and a white group to then score a hit version.

Charles Laughton, the overweight, many-chinned character actor, was announcing that he was a fill-in for Ed Sullivan, who was recuperating from a head-on car crash. Laughton, his British accent sounding to this South Carolina girl like a mixture of knowledge and honey, informed the audience that the next performer, Elvis Presley, was not actually in the New York studio, but in the CBS studio in Hollywood, where he had been filming his first movie.

"Away to Hollywood to meet Elvis Presley!" Laughton announced. A grand, dramatic flourish for this singer nobody *I* knew had ever heard of.

The camera settled on a young man wearing a plaid jacket that looked a little like our everyday tablecloth. He started in on "Don't Be Cruel." I was taking in his face—the alertness, the joy there—and wondering why in the world anyone would ever be cruel to him. The camera danced above his waist, teased us with glowing close-ups of his face, occasionally dipped far enough down to show his fingers picking his guitar.

Were those screams from the audience? I couldn't see who was screaming, and I didn't know what the unnamable urgency was, but it was pretty obvious Elvis Presley was doing something to get the girls in the theater riled up.

The brown, green, and orange afghan knitted by Grandma Kurtz covered my pajama legs and slippered feet, covered Mattie's white-nyloned legs and polished white work shoes. Every now and then, she patted my arm or knee. I slid closer to her. Elvis was definitely crossing a line. This white boy was singing Black. I recognized this. I knew that Mattie recognized it, too. We both understood.

---

Other acts by other performers followed. But they were a blur. We couldn't concentrate because Charles Laughton had told us Elvis would return later in the program. We took a break and went to the kitchen for Cokes and potato chips. We didn't need to waste our time watching anybody but Elvis. I grabbed the Charles Chips can from the pantry, scooped some into a little bowl for us to share; Mattie poured the drinks.

Now we were back on the sofa, twirling the ice in our glasses and munching noisily. Here came Elvis, singing the raucous "Ready Teddy." Then, two verses of "Hound Dog," even more raucous. The camera was now allowing us to see his whole body, from the top of his pompadoured head to the toes of his boots. The stage had completely let go of him. It couldn't contain him and his wild jig. But whenever his legs and hips started convulsing like a storm rolling in, the camera quickly switched to a close-up of his face.

The girls in the audience were screaming even louder now. I could see the way he leered at something or someone off to the side, but then he turned back to Mattie and me with a quick flash of a smile. Sometimes he just halted everything for a few seconds, stood perfectly still. Time stopped. The world stopped. We didn't move closer to tomorrow. Nobody anywhere got any older. When he did that freeze thing, it drove the audience crazy. Their screams moved decibels up the scale. I was almost too afraid to look. *I* could easily have gone crazy over that freeze thing.

Not long after Elvis appeared on *The Ed Sullivan Show,* my friend's older sister and her boyfriend drove my friend and me, along with a third friend—five of us in his brand new '56 Chevy—to see Elvis perform at the Charlotte Coliseum. Charlotte might be only twenty-six miles from Rock Hill, but seeing Elvis—seeing him *in person!*—was constellations away from our ordinary, day-to-day lives. The car shook and shivered with our excitement.

And then we were inside the Coliseum, a great, domed structure that could have whirled in from a distant planet and flopped down on busy Independence Boulevard.

We found our seats. Amazing seats, close to the stage. The lights came on. Glassy, flashing lights. Coming and going. Dark. Light. Dark. Light. Strobes roving all over us.

And then. Elvis! Onstage! Right there! Igniting the entire place!

In that minute, I thought of Mattie. If she'd been with me, we would have been screaming, pumping our arms, swaying as though we could pass out any minute. But Mattie coming with us was out of the question; you did not see a single Black face in the entire place. What was *not* out of the question was how devotedly she would listen the next morning when I told her every detail.

"I wish you'd been there, Mattie," I said. She did not say how much she wished the same. That, too, would have been out of the question. She would never express a desire to enter any world she knew was closed off to her.

But here's the truth about our family and music:

Brenda watched *Your Hit Parade,* a line-up of white stars singing pastel songs. Donald was in love with Dixieland jazz, had collected records for years, was barely a teenager when he gave a series of jazz talks to Mother's music club. My parents' taste in music? They watched *The Lawrence Welk Show.* I don't need to say another word about that. Mattie and I were the only ones in the family who knew what real music was.

# 37

In 1957, Donald was a PFC in the Army, stationed at Fort Jackson in Columbia. (After basic training, he would be stationed in Vietnam; this was after the French occupation had ended and before the war started.)

While he was at Fort Jackson, he became good friends with another PFC in his company, a Black guy from New Jersey. It had been nine years since the military had desegregated, only three years since all-Black units were eliminated. During a phone call, Donald told our parents he wanted to bring his friend home for dinner and to spend the night. The friend was so far from his family; it would be nice for him to have a home-cooked meal, sleep in a comfortable bed.

Without hesitation, our parents said yes. I don't remember any discussion about it between them or among us. I don't remember whether anyone mentioned the key thing about our guest to Mattie. I do remember that a Black person having dinner and spending the night in a white person's home was as rare in Rock Hill as an earthquake. I had never heard of such a thing. But my mother and Mattie went about preparing for the evening, as though what was about to happen was absolutely normal.

Except for this: Our breakfast room had one window, large panes overlooking the side yard and our neighbors' side yard, no more than a hundred feet from *their* window in *their* breakfast room. The man next door was a lawyer, a very conservative lawyer.

Just before Donald and his friend were to arrive, Mother pulled the curtains tight in our breakfast room. In all the years we'd lived there, those curtains had never been closed.

What I remember from the dinner: my parents, Brenda and me, Donald and his friend around the table, talking, laughing, Donald and the friend telling funny stories about the Army, the curtained window whispering *let's keep this private, we don't want any trouble,* the built-in corner cupboard holding its breath, the friend seemingly totally comfortable and relaxed, making me wonder how Black and white people got along in New Jersey, if it were as different from South Carolina as this was making me think it was.

And then, my attention turned to Mattie. She was acting very peculiar, and I wasn't sure why. She was not someone who hid her feelings; you could usually read her face. Not tonight. Was she angry? There *was* that scolding expression as she served the food, her eyes flickering left and right, then cast down, as though she wanted to break and run. She snapped the platters and bowls down on the table, stomped back into the kitchen, yes, definitely stomped, let the door separating the breakfast room from the kitchen, the door that always stayed open, she let it swing back and forth on its own, the squeaks less and less, until it finally came to a stop, shut. And when it was time to clear the table, she pushed that door open with a wham, cleared the table, did not say a word, unusual for her not to say *something,* picked up the plates, stacked them, she never stacked them, but she sure was stacking them tonight, back to the kitchen, then back into the breakfast room, cleared the serving platters, brought in a tiered plate of the peanut butter fudge she and Brenda had made, put a stack of little dessert plates in front of Mother, letting her know that she could just pass around those plates herself.

The next day, after Donald and his friend had left, after my father had gone to the store, after Mother had dropped Mattie off somewhere, maybe to one of the funerals she was always attending, maybe a doctor's appointment, Mother and Brenda and I sat in the den and talked about Mattie's reaction the night before, wondering what in the world she had been thinking. Not one of us had asked her. Not until years later, when I was grown and married, did I ask Mattie what she felt that night.

*Confused* is a word she used, working her way into her answer. *Old-fashioned*—how she described herself. She said what had gone through her head that evening was that Donald's friend had some nerve to sit and eat in a white family's home, sleep on their sheets, use the same bathroom Brenda and I used. She couldn't understand how the rest of us could act as though nothing out of the ordinary was happening, when, clearly, something was taking place that was way out of the ordinary. And just not right.

"I didn't know anything like that was even possible," she finally said. "I wasn't ready for it."

# 38

After our daughter, Laurie, was born in 1969, Mattie spent a week with Henry and me in our very cute rented duplex. Mother drove over from Rock Hill often, to hold the baby, to see how we were doing, but she did not stay with us. She thought Mattie would be more support, since she could not only help take care of our newborn, but also—unlike Mother—cook.

Mattie and I bathed Laurie in her yellow plastic tub perched on the kitchen counter. We sudsed her scalp—big bubbles!—to look like the hair it would take years for her to grow. We took turns pushing the carriage on afternoon walks, down Wonderwood Lane, up Hunter Lane, the two of us solving the world's problems, as we'd always done, a perfect loop. Mattie fed Laurie milky rice cereal with the tiny silver spoon we'd received as a baby gift. ("Rice cereal is how you get a baby to sleep through the night," she said. And she was right.) When Mother came to pick up Mattie and take her back to Rock Hill, when it was time to tell Mattie good-bye, I cried, not because I was afraid of taking care of a baby without her, but because I just did not want her to leave. I swung between a lightness—this sweet little baby now in our lives—and a sadness over the absence of Mattie in the rooms of our duplex.

Before our son, Mike, was born in 1972—I was maybe two months pregnant—Henry and I asked Mattie to be the baby's godmother. We loved the melodic high of her response—"Oh yes, yes indeed!" Then she said what she always said if plans for the future were involved: "If I be livin'." She was only fifty-four, but she always talked as if death were in the next room.

Days after we brought Mike home from the hospital, the three of us—Henry, Mattie, and I—stood together next to the sliding glass doors in the den of our very ordinary brick split-level on Lansing Drive. The doors were open to the warm afternoon. I held Mike, bundled in a soft, striped blanket, in my arms. We were surrounded by my parents, Henry's mother (Henry's dad had died the year before), the rest of our family, close friends, all gathered for Mike's bris. I wore a dark, tentlike dress that was practically a bathrobe, but it was the best I could fit into. I wanted Mattie to wear a pretty dress, something special, but she was intent on wearing her white uniform and apron.

Mattie, Henry, and I were touching, just barely, shoulder to shoulder to shoulder. The mohel, an elderly Jewish man trained and ordained to perform circumcisions, who undoubtedly had brought generations of young parents and proud grandparents bittersweet joy, was *too* elderly for the task. Henry's mother, Orthodox in her beliefs, had insisted that a mohel—not a urologist—do the job. Because she was recently widowed, and demanding, and because in those days even grown children did what their parents told them to do, we went along with her. But it was against Henry's and my better judgment. And now I was seeing the mohel's trembling hands, his tentative balance. When I look back on that moment, I think it was too much like a *Saturday Night Live* skit to be funny. Who invited Dan Ackroyd to perform our son's bris? I was scared to death.

A small cloth-covered table separated Henry, Mattie, and me (and Mike) from the rabbi and the mohel and his knife. The rabbi uttered prayers in Hebrew and in English, took our sweet baby, placed him on the table, dabbed his lips with a gauze pad soaked in red wine to numb the pain of what was about to be done. The mohel opened the blanket, and signaled for Henry to hold the baby's legs still. The mohel then did what he'd been trained to do God knows how many decades before. I couldn't look; Mattie inched closer to me. The baby was crying a really frantic cry. Was the wine just symbolic? It was not numbing his pain.

The rabbi bundled the baby back up and asked, "Who is the godmother?"

Mattie proudly took a step forward, chin up, and declared over the baby's cries, "I'm the godmother."

The rabbi then handed her the baby and offered a few more prayers, and the bris was over.

Our house might have been ordinary, but what was not ordinary is this: how Mattie softened the harshness of the day. She immediately tunneled that baby close to her ample bosom, gave him her pinkie finger, he latched on with his tiny mouth still glistening with wine, his cries grew quieter and quieter, until they stopped.

The rest of the afternoon, Mattie held Mike—"We're not puttin' this baby down. No sir. He needs comforting." She sat in the rocker in the den, people milling around, chatting with her, oohing and aahing over the baby, and she just held him close. Back and forth, back and forth, the two of them rocked. If he'd been old enough to hum, he would have.

---

Twenty-six years later, the summer of 1998, Mike and Brooke were married on top of a mountain. Just before Brooke's grandparents, Mattie walked slowly down the grassy aisle, wearing a pink silk dress with a matching jacket, a rose corsage, and an unearthly angel smile. Normally, right before the bride's grandparents, it would have been my parents and Henry's parents *and* Mattie, but our parents were no longer living and Mattie was doing just fine in her role, and Henry and I both were deeply grateful for her presence.

Brooke's family sat in folding white chairs on one side of the aisle; on the other, Henry, Mattie, and me. (Laurie was a bridesmaid, and Bob, the young man she would marry the following summer, was a groomsman.) At one point during the ceremony, I glanced over at Mattie. Even in the blurred light of early evening, I could see tears leaking from behind her eyelids, just like mine. It felt familiar and comforting, as though she and I were communicating to each other something essential.

# 39

In 1975 I was thirty-four. Mother was sixty-five, and something was terribly wrong with her. The tight, disappointed mouth. Sad eyes. Dark reserve. The pacing, from the living room to the front door and back again, a straight, anxious path. She strained to find a word, finish a sentence. Our two-way conversations were now one-way, me basically conversing with myself, coming up with all the crucial details:

"Um . . . she came by . . . um . . ." Mother trying to tell me something.

"Somebody came to see you? That's really nice. Who was it?" Me, trying to get the story.

"You know . . . that person . . ."

"Now, which person was that? Somebody we know in Rock Hill?"

"Yes, she came . . . um . . . somebody I haven't seen in a long time . . . what-d'ya-call-it? . . . you know who I'm . . . uh . . . talking about . . ."

"You mean _____?" (Fill in the blank with what will be many guesses.)

The first time I'd noticed the change was when my mother-in-law was visiting from Miami and talking with Mother and me over chicken sandwiches at my kitchen table about the possibility of moving into a condominium. "If you move into a *condonimium*—" Mother said. Then she said it again. *Condonimium.* She kept saying it. She knew it wasn't right, but she couldn't make those consonants behave. I remember thinking, *Why can't Mother—an intelligent, articulate person—say this simple, ordinary word?*

Alzheimer's disease.

My father declared that as long as Mother knew where she was, she would remain at home. He would not think of moving her into a nursing home until she became unaware of her surroundings. Brenda, Donald, Mattie, and I totally agreed with this decision.

Mattie made my father's plan work. She cooked the foods Mother loved, coaxed her to eat, helped her get dressed, reminded her to bathe. When it became necessary, Mattie bathed her and dressed her and fed her. When Mother's friends began dropping away—as friends do in these circumstances—Mattie was who she'd always been: Mother's best friend.

---

Early one morning, in 1979, my father called. His voice was calm. Well, maybe the right word for how he sounded is *bewildered.* "Mother is worse," he said. "Much worse. I don't know, I just don't know." He said she couldn't speak at all. She didn't know where she was or who he was or who Mattie was.

Had she experienced a stroke, or was it just one of those plunges Alzheimer's patients take? We would never know.

I immediately called Brenda, and we drove to Rock Hill together, to the house our parents had built on the outskirts of town after I'd graduated from college. On the way, we talked about what was going on, what this meant, what we would do. But we did not say the thing that was truest: *Our mother is near the end.*

The two of us walked into the kitchen. Mother was wearing her robe, open to her nightgown, sash untied, her silver hair a bird's nest of tangles from the night before or from whatever had gone on before we got there. She sat at the little square table, her face so close to the plate you'd think she was half-blind. She was eating pancakes with her hands, syrup dripping down her wrists. Every now and then, she made a sound like a hollow growl. You might have thought she had something caught in her throat. But she did not. She never looked up at us. Nothing existed but those pancakes and how many she could stuff into her mouth. Mattie was sitting right next to her, inches away, holding a cloth napkin, dabbing when she could get a dab in. I know Mattie was thinking, *What on earth can I do that might possibly help, up against this?*

Mattie got Mother cleaned up and dressed in the loose-fitting knit pants and tops she now wore, elastic waist, easy to pull on and off, not the beautiful and stylish clothes she used to wear. Brenda and I half-walked, half-carried her out to our father's car.

As our father shifted into reverse and we backed down the driveway, I could see Mattie at the top of the driveway, just standing there, not moving, watching us, watching over us.

Mother's mind had been jerked loose. Brenda and I held her in the back seat, as she ricocheted from one side of the car to the other. Her growls grew louder and louder. My lips were so dry I had to keep wetting them with my tongue. We held our mother, while our father drove just under the speed limit to the hospital in Charlotte. Cars zoomed by. We begged him to drive faster—it was so hard to keep Mother from hurting herself as she threw her small body around—but he didn't believe in breaking the law, so he drove five miles under the speed limit. A steady 60 mph.

There was nothing the doctors in the hospital could do for her but medicate her, and then, days later, discharge her. She went from the hospital bed to a nursing home bed.

For two years, she lay there, drugged, unable to speak, barely able to move, guard rails locked to keep her in. Our father moved to Charlotte, staying with Brenda and Chuck, then with Henry and me, so that he could spend all day, every day, at Mother's side. He, too, was dying—of colon cancer, metastasized to his lungs, bones, and brain. Radiation treatments were keeping him going. Radiation treatments, and looking after Mother.

About once a week, Brenda or I drove to Rock Hill to pick up Mattie and bring her to Charlotte. She was retired now, although she kept watch over my parents' house, checking in every now and then, cleaning what needed to be cleaned. My father still paid her as though she were working full-time.

At the nursing home, Mattie sat by Mother's bed, her chair close to my father's chair, their knees touching the mattress, my father and Mattie joined in caring for Mother. Mattie rubbed Mother's legs with the English Lavender lotion she'd brought from Mother's bedside table at home. She brushed her hair, talked to her, talked, talked, all those memories the two of them shared. And she sang to her, sweet gospel hymns. Mattie's voice choked from time to time, but I believe the music she made reached Mother, through her skin or her muscles or her bones.

# 40

I was in my forties when I started asking Mattie if she would take me to church with her one Sunday.

Both my parents were gone; Mattie was enjoying full retirement, attending church conferences all over the country, going on Caribbean cruises with Minnie, the two of them flying to California to visit Mattie's granddaughters and great-grandchildren. (Flying together made them less afraid of plane travel.) Mattie also took oil painting classes. (Always artistic, she used to decorate the grocery-list chalkboard in our kitchen with intricate floral designs.)

Donald, Brenda, and I now paid her every week. Before my father died, he had discussed Mattie's financial situation with us, and we decided the best plan was for the three of us to support her for the rest of her life. I know this sounds paternalistic, but it seemed a better idea than our parents leaving Mattie a lump sum. What if she lived a long time and her money ran out? She might not tell us. We begged her to spend money: *Don't save it, Mattie!* We made sure her checking account could cover anything she would need or want. Once, when Mattie came to me and said she wanted to give a large sum of money to her sister, Ethel, who was struggling financially, we made a $5,000 deposit into Mattie's checking account so that she could help her sister. The arrangement worked well for all of us.

—◦◦◦◦—

I knew how involved Mattie was in St. Matthews AME Zion Church in Rock Hill. Members of the congregation called her

Mother Culp. We shopped together for white lacy dresses for ushering; I picked out Easter outfits as gifts for her at Belk in Charlotte, light-colored silk dresses, always with a matching jacket, in case the weather turned cool. Looking back, it's amazing to me that I could so easily select clothes for her. I usually brought several dresses to her house, so that, together, we could pick the perfect one. She'd stand before the full-length mirror hanging on the back of her closet door, reach out and tap it lightly on the side to straighten it. Then she'd turn, one way, the other, look over her shoulder—the only time I ever saw her openly admire herself. We'd scrutinize each outfit. Skirt too short. Jacket a little snug. Or neckline just right. Sleeves perfect. The color, the fit—yes, this one.

Obviously, I was not a child at this point, but I was still petitioning her as though I were: "Please, Mattie, I really want to go to church with you."

I knew some of her church friends. I'd met her minister at her house once. The only thing missing was being with her in the place that meant so much to her, the two of us sitting close in her regular pew, my legs crossed like hers, both of us nodding *yes, that's right* along with the minister's sermon, sharing a hymnal, our voices dropping and rising.

She always answered something like, "We gon' do that. We definitely gon' do that. I'll take you one Sunday soon."

But that Sunday never came.

I'd ask again, certain it was just a matter of finding the *right* Sunday.

Again, she promised she'd make that happen.

Surely, our connected lives meant we should share that part of her life. I thought it was a perfectly reasonable request.

I don't really know what it was to her.

But she was not a person who would just forget to take care of something. If she made a promise, she kept the promise. It did not make sense that I asked, she said okay, and then nothing happened.

One explanation: Maybe she thought I was just being polite. But really, she knew me better than that. If I asked to go, it meant I wanted to go.

Maybe she believed it would be improper of her to take me. Improper to put me in that situation. White people didn't go to Black churches in the 1980s. *Bless Judy's heart. But it's just not done. Judy might feel uncomfortable. The only white person in the whole place. Lord, I can't do that.*

Or could it have been Mattie's own discomfort she was sidestepping? She would never have wanted to do anything to call attention to herself. I can imagine the stares she would have received, bringing me into that sanctuary. Too much?

My thoughts go to my parents and how Mattie might have felt if they knew she had taken me to her church. I'm certain they would have been fine with it. But taking me to church could have felt to Mattie the same as sitting down with our family at the dinner table. Too modern. Too unfamiliar. Not okay. She and my parents were of the same generation, and Mattie could have mistakenly believed they'd feel the same way she did. No matter how many times Mattie might draw and redraw the scene, she wouldn't be able to bring it into focus. It could seem like stepping through a wall. Cracking sheetrock.

Another explanation for why her yes meant no might have been that at church, she was a different person. In other parts of her life, she was a domestic worker—a maid, a cook. Inside those hallowed walls, she was *somebody.* Prominent. A person of stature. Maybe she could not blend those two Matties in her mind. A distinguished elder in the church acting like a maid bringing her white child along with her.

Time after time, she'd been honored by the congregation. How proudly she had shown Mother and me and then, in later years, Henry and me, the programs from those events. She'd even had a formal studio photograph taken, and that stylish picture —her dazzling smile, curly wig, sparkling red blouse, dangly earrings

—appeared on the cover of many programs. We loved hearing the details, what people said to her, how the minister praised her from the pulpit. What would it be like for her if I witnessed firsthand all that acclaim? She was not accustomed to standing out in any world the two of us inhabited. In the sphere of my childhood, I had always been the center. Would she have had trouble finding a place for me in an environment where she was the center?

And then there's the matter of how my presence could have compromised Sunday morning for her, felt burdensome, pulled her out of herself, when in herself is exactly where she wanted to be. Not in a self-centered way. Never in a self-centered way. Just in that way that prayer can feel personal. Intimate. Private.

Maybe she just did not want me with her. Not *there*. In that sanctuary.

How did I feel about being turned down? I never thought it *wouldn't* happen. Next week. The week after. I really believed it was only a matter of time before I'd drive to Rock Hill to pick her up, the two of us dressed in our Sunday best.

After Mattie had been gone for years—in 2019—I asked Pernettia, who was now ninety-one, why she thought Mattie did not take me to church with her.

"Let me think how to say this," Pernettia said. It was at the end of a long phone conversation. She didn't sound as though she was *reluctant* to voice her opinion. It was more that she wanted to find the precise explanation. "I believe Mattie might think it was— what's the right word?—*awkward,* if people started standing up and doing all kinds of things in the middle of church and if the preacher started yelling, instead of just talking. You know, sometimes that went on in that church. Mattie would worry how it might feel to you."

In the end, I had to learn that our partnership could go just so far. And the only time I ever set foot in her church was for her funeral.

# 41

It was 1998, Mattie was eighty, and Henry and I wanted to make sure that Minnie would inherit Mattie's house, her possessions, and the money in her checking account. We took Mattie to a lawyer in Rock Hill to draw up her will. The lawyer used to live across from us on Eden Terrace. (He was the little boy who appeared at our front door when tasty things were being taken out of the oven.) I knew Mattie would feel comfortable meeting with him. Henry and I planned to take care of his fee.

When it came time to pay, the lawyer put his arm around Mattie's shoulders and said, grinning widely, "Heck, I've known you my whole life, Mattie. I practically teethed on the peanut butter fudge and candy apples you and Brenda made. There's no way I could charge you." And then he added, with an even wider grin, "Of course, those candy apples just about broke my front teeth!"

"But *we're* paying," Henry said.

"It's Mattie's will, and it's my gift to Mattie."

I tell this part because I like showing her effect on *everyone*.

———∞———

But now, where was the will? I thought it was a good thing for me to know where it was, in case I needed to put my hands on it. She agreed.

I was standing on her dressing table bench, rummaging through the top shelf in her closet. She was sitting on the edge of her bed, telling me how to shift the hats and pocketbooks around so that I could find the shoebox that held the will.

And then. There it was. A shoebox tucked in the hollow of a black wool hat.

I stepped down from the bench, slid it back under the dressing table, and lifted the top off the shoebox. Yes, there was the will, just as she'd promised. But underneath it was—what? Insurance policies? I leafed through them. There were maybe fifteen or twenty.

"What are these?" I asked, holding the box and the will in one hand and waving a couple of the insurance policies in the other, their gold embossed seals catching the light.

"Oh, never mind," she said quickly, rising from the bed, taking the policies and the box out of my hand, leaving me with the will. "You don't need to worry none about that."

"But," I said, "who do all these insurance policies belong to?"

"It's just somethin' for my burial. Somethin' I take care of." She'd already put everything back in the box, lid on, fastened securely, all four corners. Holding the box tight under her arm, she started dragging the bench over to the closet. This eighty-year-old woman was getting ready to climb up on the bench to put the shoebox back on that high shelf.

"Wait!" I said. "Mattie!"

Somehow, I convinced her to let me take the box home to show Henry the insurance policies. If I just mentioned Henry's name, it lent legitimacy to whatever I was proposing.

But she was not happy with me.

Of course, she liked things to stay the same. Mattie was the grown-up, the one who decided what was what—particularly, what I should and shouldn't do. I was the child, who did what she said.

That night, as Henry and I studied the policies, we discovered that they had been taken out so long ago, they were all paid up. Had been paid up for years. Yet it was clear the insurance companies were continuing to send agents around to collect, and she was continuing to pay. Thousands of dollars paid, when zero was due.

The next day Henry called our insurance agent to ask how to proceed. He said what we were seeing was not all that unusual, that there were some barely legitimate companies that sold policies to people who were "uneducated or elderly or just not aware." The companies could keep collecting long past the dates the policies were paid off. In fact, they would collect until the person died. That's the reason many of these policies were taken out—to pay for the policyholder's burial. Our insurance agent suggested that we write a letter to each company, cash in all the policies, collect as much of the money owed to Mattie as we could.

I felt disheartened, so very disheartened. I dreaded starting the process, not because of the work involved, but because here it was again: a reminder of how things were. What our insurance agent was *not* saying: Black people were often the victims of these scams. Once again, I could not save Mattie from being mistreated by the world.

When I explained to her what we were about to do, she trusted me enough to say okay. But while I was trying to give something back to her, I was also taking something away: Her pride in being able to handle her own affairs. Her ability to make decisions, including financial decisions. Take care of business. I was loosening something she had worked hard to fasten tight.

One of the things she told me was that she knew these insurance salesmen. They were white men who came to her house every quarter—sometimes, monthly—to collect. "Real nice men," she said. "They always come in and sit and visit. I fix iced tea, we talk, they show me pictures in their wallets, I been lookin' at pictures of their children and grandchildren so long they grown up now. Goodness, I can't even think how many years I been knowin' these men."

———&oogsco;———

There were no addresses on the policies. So Henry and I went to work, researching (pre-Internet for us), following leads. Finally, we found addresses for the different companies.

I wrote a sample letter, which I copied and mailed to each company.

No replies.

Now we needed phone numbers. More research.

We followed up our letters with calls. Sometimes there was no answer. Sometimes, voice mail. Sometimes we got a receptionist, but she wouldn't put us through to anyone. We left messages, and nobody called us back. Finally, we reached a salesman. Then another, and another. But they would not own up. We spoke with their supervisors. Still, nobody owned up. We threatened lawsuits.

In the end, we were able to cash in all the policies and collect most of the money these crooks had taken from Mattie.

Because the beneficiary in each policy was Minnie, we asked Mattie whether we should give the checks we were collecting to her or to Minnie.

Minnie, she said.

Mattie thanked Henry and me. Told us over and over how blessed she was to have children who took such good care of her. But I could tell she was not happy with me.

Was she holding on to the snapshot memory of those policies tucked inside the black wool hat on her closet shelf, how they represented security? The security of a paid-in-full burial?

*Oh,* I thought, *that's easy.* I then promised her she would have the burial she wanted.

But the burial was only part of it. The insurance policies also represented a final gift to her daughter. Something that Mattie, and only Mattie, could make happen. She must have imagined Minnie's surprise, after Mattie's death, when Minnie would receive all that insurance money. Instead, I was the one who handed it over to Minnie. Of course, the way those fraudulent insurance companies operated, it is doubtful Minnie would have gotten a dime. Still, in Mattie's mind, not only were the policies canceled; her last chance to take care of her daughter was also canceled.

# 42

And the years passed. Sun, then shadow. Mattie grew older. And weaker. She took in her older sister, Emma Lee, who seemed to be in better shape than she was, but Mattie cooked for Emma Lee and cared for her. Mattie even moved into the guest room and gave Emma Lee the master bedroom. I begged Mattie to move back into her own room and let Emma Lee take care of *her*. But she relied on the fact that her sister was older and, therefore, needed her help.

And then one night, in 2006, Mattie was getting out of bed to use the bathroom. Just as she slid off the bed and her feet touched the carpet, she realized her legs were not going to support her. She fell. Hard. Broke her ankle.

Days in a rehab hospital. Home again. Emma Lee's very pleasant nephew came to live with them. He promised me that the thing he wanted most in the world—because they'd been so good to him— was to help Mattie and Emma Lee. But he ended up helping himself to Mattie's cash and other things around the house until, finally, I convinced Mattie he should find some other place to live.

Then, months of calm. A honeyed lapse. Mattie seemed to be rousing herself back to life, growing stronger. I felt hopeful.

But the world was not going to be reshaped at this point. What I couldn't bear were the days *between* when I was able to drive over for a visit, to help a little. The gaps. That's where my worry gathered. It was Mattie who finally acknowledged she could no longer take care of herself. Or Emma Lee. Mattie was ready to move into a nursing home. It was early 2007, and she had just turned eighty-nine.

Minnie, still living in New York City, was traveling to Rock Hill as often she could, every few months. But her daughter and grandson were now living with her, and she needed to babysit while her daughter taught school. Minnie and I were in contact by phone. It was time for us to discuss Mattie's next step. I did research and visited all the places in Rock Hill. The very nicest one—with both white and Black residents—had an opening. Donald, Chuck, Henry, and I would take care of the costs not covered by Mattie's insurance. (Brenda had died of bile duct cancer the year before. The morning after Brenda died, Mattie told me, "Brenda came to me in a dream last night, and we had a nice visit. I don't need to go to her funeral. I can't take it." I understood.)

The day Henry and I moved Mattie in, I knew I'd chosen the right place. She already knew practically everyone who worked there. Nurses, physical therapists, aides, and housekeepers poked their heads in her room to welcome her. "Mother Culp," they called her. "Do you need anything, Mother Culp? What can I do for you?" I don't remember if the sun was shining that day. Inside, it was all light and bright. Mattie, Henry, and I joked and laughed with everyone, as though the days ahead were full of promise.

The only not-so-bright part of those first hours: Her roommate, a Black woman, *seemed* pretty normal. (Not unusual, even in 2006, for Black people to room only with Black people, whites with whites.) However, at random times, she would just let out a howl, loud and animal-like, so loud it could rattle the pictures off the wall, if there'd been pictures on the wall. Then she would seem normal again. A howl, a shock each time. I could not let this be. I felt sorry for the woman, but I'd promised Mattie I would take care of her. A howling roommate was not part of the promise. I marched into the resident manager's office and explained why Mattie had to be moved; he saw how resolute I was, and she was immediately moved to a different room.

Mattie's new roommate was a quiet, gentle woman, tiny, delicate, not able to get out of bed at all, but her mind was sharp, and she and Mattie enjoyed each other right from the beginning. Even though the two of them had never met, Mattie knew her people. But then, Mattie knew most everybody's people.

She settled in, marking her place clearly, making herself at home.

For a while, Emma Lee lived in Mattie's house. Then her children moved her into the same nursing home as Mattie—two sisters down the hall from one another. Mattie's house was now unoccupied. Henry and I checked on it from time to time. Ethel, Mattie's sister, made sure her son cut the grass.

Sometimes I brought Bojangles' fried chicken for Mattie, her roommate, and Emma Lee. Bojangles' was Mattie's new favorite, as though she had not been widely known for her own home-cooked fried chicken. I'd wheel Emma Lee into Mattie's room, and the four of us would eat those crispy drumsticks, biscuits, and fries, then lick our fingers clean. Once, *I* fried chicken legs to take to them, but Mattie pretended, even though my chicken was fine (of course, she would say it was more than fine—*delicious! perfect!*), that she really liked Bojangles' better. She was still trying to make life easy for me. *Too much trouble to cook, child. You can buy it just as good.*

Sometimes I took her out for a drive. My eyes on the road, I'd take a quick peek over at her. You'd think I was driving her straight to Paris. That's how radiant she appeared, the anticipation, the openness of the day. We always ended up at the cafeteria we both loved. We filled our plates with steamed squash, fried okra, cornbread, banana pudding.

When the afternoons were warm, I wheeled her onto the back patio of the nursing home, flowerbeds surrounding us, insects buzzing, sunlight scalloping the oaks. She would drape a cardigan over her shoulders, in case there was a breeze. We'd share a Coke and a small bag of potato chips.

This period of time was a swirl of small, lovely moments and scares. She would suddenly become short of breath, just lying in bed; her feet and ankles would swell so much, they looked like they could burst. Diagnosis: congestive heart failure. Each flare-up took her by ambulance to the hospital, where she'd stay a couple of days, sometimes longer, stripped of all that made her Mattie. She'd lie in that hospital bed, all stillness and silence. I was by her side, feeling like the ground was breaking. But then she'd rally, feel much better, more like herself, be discharged back to the nursing home, where we'd have more small, lovely moments. Until the next scare.

---

Early in the morning on Labor Day 2007, Ethel called.

"She's gone."

She was eighty-nine.

I hung up the phone from Ethel and immediately called out to Henry, "We've got to go! Quick!" I threw on my jeans and shirt, combed my hair, pushed Henry to get dressed fast, hurry, hurry, we need to get there, as soon as we can, right now, let's go, come on!

But:

Why am I rushing to her? Am I thinking I can save her? Bring her back, take care of her? Tell her one last thing? Kiss her cheek one more time? No. It's over. We don't need to go.

I called Ethel back. "Is there anything I can do to help? Do you want me to come?"

"No, dear, you don't need to come. We're doing all right. Can I do anything for you?"

Do anything for me? Naturally, she would ask this. I was Mattie's baby and her job was to take care of me. Not the other way around. Mattie's sister would fall right in with that way of thinking. We were back to how it all began. She'd think it was too forward to say she needed me. Whatever had to be done, she would assure me she was taking care of it.

I was shaking. I could hear my own breathing. I was weak with wanting Mattie. I sank into a chair, and this thought came to me as though I were seeing things clearly for the first time: *Labor Day. Mattie's labor is done.*

# 43

Minnie wrote the obituary for the funeral program. On the cover: Mattie's studio photograph, taken years before—her dazzling smile, curly wig, sparkling red blouse, dangly earrings.

> *Mattie Culp was one of eleven children, born on February 26, 1918, in Chester, South Carolina, to the late Benny and Addie Cherry. She died on Monday, September 3, 2007.*
>
> *She attended the Liberty Hill School in Catawba, South Carolina, and at an early age she joined Bethel A.M.E. Zion Church in Landsford. She moved to Rock Hill in 1944 and became employed by the beloved Kurtz family. She stayed with this family many years and considered them a part of her family. Mattie joined St. Matthews A.M.E. Zion Church, where she became an active member, serving as an Usher, Missionary Worker, Choir Member, and Kitchen Supervisor, until ill health forced her to resign from many of her duties. She was a Church Mother and was affectionately known all over St. Matthews as "Mother Culp."*
>
> *She leaves to cherish her memory, one daughter, Minnie Callender; three granddaughters, Linda Callender Williams, Michelle Callender Diggs (Shelton), and Lauren Callender Hightower; six great-grandchildren, Kristin Callender, Joseph Elie, Sasha Elie, Veronicah Williams, Brandon Williams, and*

*John Laurence Hightower; two brothers, George Cherry (Louise) and Harold Cherry; two sisters, Emma Lee Barber and Ethel Agurs; one sister-in-law, Delores Cherry; Judy Goldman (Henry) and the entire Kurtz Family; and a host of nieces, nephews, cousins, and friends.*

# 44

The six of us—Henry and I, Laurie and Bob, Mike and Brooke—drove together to St. Matthews A.M.E. Zion Church on Lige Street in Rock Hill, a simple, red brick building with a white steeple, the church Mattie did not take me to.

And even though I'd never been there before, the minute I entered the sanctuary, that physical space, I felt her everywhere.

I sat between Henry and Pernettia. I was glad to be close to Pernettia. It felt as though the length of my body wanted to be in contact with the length of hers.

Laurie and Bob, Mike and Brooke sat on the other side of Henry. Donald, Chuck, his four sons, David, Brian, Scott, and Danny, were in the pew behind us. I leaned forward and smiled at Laurie and Mike, looked over my shoulder and smiled at Brenda's sons, thought of all that Mattie had meant to these six children—the way love for her roped its way through the generations, like a vine between tree branches. They thought of Mattie as their grandmother. She had cared for each one as a newborn just home from the hospital, held them, unhesitatingly and sure. She had stayed with them whenever Brenda and Chuck or Henry and I went out of town. The holidays she spent with our families. Thanksgiving. Passover. Birthdays, graduations, weddings. One Christmas, in 1993, "the cousins," as these children called themselves even after they were grown and living in far-flung places, knew they'd all be in Charlotte for the holidays and wanted to do something special for Mattie. The phone calls back and forth, the different ideas for a gift, the debates. In the end, they decided on diamond earrings. A few days before Christmas, the six of them drove in two cars to Mattie's house in Rock Hill. (Our families, no longer celebrating Christmas, now concentrated on Hanukkah; Mattie was now spending Christmas in New York with Minnie.) One car took the wrong exit off the interstate. Oh, how the driver of that car would get ribbed by everyone in the other car! They all finally arrived at Mattie's front door. Laurie was the only female cousin. (Sasha, Donald's daughter, lived in New York and couldn't join them.) The photograph I have from that day: Mattie, big happy grin, wearing a white turtleneck, sweatshirt, paisley bandana wrapped around her head. Laurie, big happy grin, plaid flannel shirt, having already put one earring bright as a small sun in Mattie's ear, is tenderly threading the second earring into Mattie's other ear. I'm sure the next thing was Mattie saying to one of them, "Get me my hand mirror. On my dressing table, in my bedroom." And someone brought it to her and she turned her head one way, then the other, and I'm sure there were many *I'm blessed*s and they all felt the love in that room.

---

One pew ahead of me was Ethel, Mattie's younger sister. Emma Lee, her older sister, was not well enough to come. Mattie's friend, Mckie, her husband, and their daughter were beside Ethel.

Every time we sang a hymn, or whenever the minister mentioned Mattie's name, Ethel stood up, waved her arms, and called out her grief. Pernettia and I passed one ragged Kleenex back and forth between us. At one point during the service, she whispered in my ear, "Just look at Ethel. She doesn't need to carry on like that."

The weight of all that light pouring in those tall windows.

The order of the service: invocation, choir, scripture (Old Testament, New Testament), prayers, voice solo, poems read by two of Mattie's granddaughters and a great-granddaughter, piano solo, eulogy.

After the voice solo and before the poems, the minister invited anyone who wanted to say a few words to come forward. I wanted to speak, I didn't want to speak. I'd already said everything to Mattie I would ever want to say. Her words and my words were fixed forever. Let others speak. I needed to just sit and think. Life without Mattie. How would that be done?

Mattie's friends and many cousins spoke about their—our—Mattie. Chuck walked to the front of the church and said how much our family loved her. He told a few stories, some funny, all sweet. The boys who'd boarded with Mattie—now grown men—went up as a group and each told a particular memory of her. The last one talked about her cooking. He held out his hands, palms up, as if he were holding a bowl of her goodness.

At the end, the congregation stood and sang "I'll Fly Away." Ethel swayed, waved her arms. Pernettia nudged me with her elbow, cocked her head toward Ethel.

For a second, I imagined Mattie standing beside me, the two of us sharing a hymnal, our voices dropping and rising. The two of us. In her church.

⸺∞⸺

Then, the cemetery. Mattie's family and friends and my family made a wide half-circle around the opening that had been dug, red-orange South Carolina dirt mounded on one side, the coffin inches away, ready to be lowered into the earth. I stood next to Minnie. Before the service began, I reached into my pocket, took out Mattie's diamond ring and earrings, slipped them into Minnie's hand. She turned toward me and smiled a smile that let me know she knew the ring and earrings well, their history, all that they represented.

The minister was now praying. And then it was over. That was it. Done. The day suddenly so dry, even the air I breathed felt like ash.

# 45

Months after Mattie's funeral, I was at a party in Charlotte, and a woman I'd known growing up in Rock Hill wanted to tell me about getting in touch "after all these years" with the Black woman who'd raised her. This woman at the party, so proud, so in love with symbols, told me how she'd taken her former maid out to lunch, how grand she looked—now in her nineties! Imagine!

This person I'd known a long time even pulled out her cell phone to show me the selfie she'd taken of the two of them at the restaurant. How thrilled she was, after all those years, to see the person who'd taken care of her.

Here's what annoyed me: She wanted to tell me her story because she knew about my relationship with Mattie. And she was making her relationship with her Black maid parallel to mine.

Why did she let *all those years* lapse before she got in touch with her? And why just one lunch? Why didn't she know how grand the woman who'd raised her looked in her fifties, sixties, seventies, and eighties? How dare she compare their meager connection with Mattie's and my deep connection?

I'll give her this: At least she got in touch with her. But I refused to join her in talking about the women who'd raised us. I changed the subject. Focused on how pleasant the party was, the buffet, the vase of hydrangeas on the piano. Anything but this mutual interest of ours that didn't feel so mutual to me.

What I know now that I didn't know then:

That woman's story terrified me. Her description of the lunch, their selfie, this conversation coming so soon after Mattie's death made me not entirely sure what my own facts were or what they meant. I recoiled from her story because it tested what I've been telling myself *all these years.*

Can we trust anything inside the system we were brought up in? A system founded on, and still dependent on, oppression? Can I see the world as it really was, as it really is? And has it even changed that much? Black maids calming cranky white children in grocery store checkout lines. Hispanic nannies pushing white children in park swings. So many women, so many years, taking care of other women's children.

What I've finally come to: It is possible for love to co-exist with ugliness.

I understand now that I should have gone ahead and engaged in conversation with the woman at the party. What she knew to be true would not have altered what I knew to be true. Mattie and I loved each other, despite the unconscionable scaffolding on which our relationship was built. Every day with her was concrete proof of what is right in this world, even in the midst of its wrongs.

# 46

I'm sitting at my dressing table, pushing the hairbrush and comb and my little compact of blush aside so that I can look at the photograph of Mattie and me with our matching smiles, my arm around her shoulder, my hand resting there. The picture was taken in my kitchen one long-ago Thanksgiving. She's wearing her white, long-sleeved uniform. I'm wearing a white blouse with the gold and silver pin Brooke, my daughter-in-law, had given to me for my birthday. You can see a gold chain around Mattie's neck. And her diamond earrings. We stopped to pose for the camera, just before we spooned rice into the white ceramic bowl decorated with cherries that *always* held the rice on Thanksgiving, just before we poured gravy into the gravy boat, took the sweet potato casserole and cornbread dressing from the oven and placed them on the island beside the green beans we'd snapped together and the big, round platter of turkey Henry had just carved. We were about to call everyone in.

Many photographs are pressed flat under the heavy glass covering the top of this dressing table—photographs of my parents, Brenda, Donald, Henry, my children, grandchildren, close friends. But I'm concentrating on the picture of Mattie and me.

This dressing table used to be Mother's. I can still see her sitting on the cream-colored leather bench, leaning closer to the attached mirror with its scalloped edges, the light maple wood. She'd be lifting her hair off her forehead, smoothing on moisturizer, or pursing her lips to curl bright red lipstick into the corners of her mouth. She gave the dressing table and bench to Mattie when she and my father moved to their new house. From then on, the dressing table was in Mattie's house. She was the one who thought of displaying photographs under the glass. I can see Mattie situating herself on the bench, leaning closer to the mirror. She'd be powdering her face, her old-fashioned, pink, fluffy puff, the box of loose powder the exact shade of her skin, her cool, smooth, Hershey-brown skin I wrote about in my poem.

I remember saying to Mattie, when I was at her house, "Mattie, I love that you have Mother's dressing table and I want you to keep it for as long as you live. But when you die, could I have it?"

The day after Mattie's funeral, Minnie called to ask if I'd still like to have the dressing table. I was touched that Minnie was so earnestly carrying out Mattie's (my) wishes. Minnie would be in Rock Hill only a couple of days longer, then back to New York.

That afternoon, Henry and I drove over to Mattie's house for what I knew would be the last time. We parked at the curb. Henry got out of the car and walked on ahead. I went more slowly, because I wanted to take everything in.

The dogwood near the street looked healthy, still not hit by the disease that had killed most of the dogwoods across the South.

There were no pansies lining the walk; it was too early for pansies anyway, even if Mattie had still been living here. She never planted them before October, when nights grew cool.

The rose bushes over to the side, next to Delsey Mae's house, were still thriving, even without Mattie's care. Like children, they had been given a good foundation and would go on blooming without her.

I walked past the spot where fire ants had once built their very distinctive mound of loose dirt. One day when Henry and I were at Mattie's, he showed it to her, she said don't worry about it, she'd get one of the boys in the neighborhood to take care of it, she didn't want him to have to bother, he wasn't giving up though, he asked how do you get rid of fire ants, she told him you buy fire ant poison, he asked where, she told him Family Dollar, he drove there and picked up a bag, coated the area with the granules, Mattie and I sat on the porch steps and watched, she told him now you soak it with water, he dragged the hose across the lawn, waved it over the mound like a wand, turning the water into an arc that crossed itself over and over, she said keep watering, he blocked half the flow with his fingers to make it stronger, she said don't stop, those fire ants don't give up so easy, he kept on until the path to Mattie's door was clear.

------⊗⊗⊗------

I looked up. Minnie was standing on the front porch, talking with Henry. I think she'd been sitting in one of the Adirondack chairs, waiting for us.

I joined the two of them and we went inside, into the living room. Henry and I sat together on the sofa, Minnie in Mattie's oversized wing chair, the white lace doily behind her head. I glanced into the kitchen, at the *Mattie's Kitchen* sign on the wall beside the stove, each letter cut from a different gingham print. (Before Henry and I left, I asked Minnie if I could have the sign for Laurie. It still hangs in Laurie's kitchen.)

Minnie, Henry, and I talked about the funeral, how nice it was, the music, the minister's eulogy, how Mattie would have been pleased with everyone's comments about her but never would have said it.

At some point, Minnie brought out a pitcher of iced tea, which was not as sweet or lemony as Mattie's, but still good.

I didn't know this would be the last time I would see Minnie. Fourteen months later, at age seventy-four, she would die of a heart attack. The sad irony: Mattie left Minnie when she was small, and now Mattie leaves her again. Minnie would not survive this one.

Minnie led Henry and me through the hall, past the mahogany telephone table that used to sit in the back hall beside the kitchen in our house on Eden Terrace. The little table held Mattie's beige phone, and the thin Rock Hill phone book on the shelf beneath the seat.

Past the photographs hanging high on the wall: Minnie in her cap and gown. Mattie's granddaughters and great-grandchildren. My parents, Donald, Brenda, and me, our children and grandchildren. A birthday letter I'd written to Mattie, which she had framed. A formal studio photograph of Grandma Kurtz, who'd taught Mattie how to "cook Jewish." Once, I took a friend with me to visit Mattie, and my friend told me later that, considering the pictures on the walls, if you didn't know better, you'd think you were in a white person's house.

Henry and I followed Minnie into the small guest room Mattie had insisted on sleeping in so that Emma Lee could have the larger master bedroom. The guest room looked the same as it had the day we moved Mattie into the nursing home. On the chest of drawers, a tiny bottle of perfume, roll-on deodorant, things I should've taken to her, but didn't. A wide-brimmed, feathered church hat hung on the closet doorknob. The mirror on the back of the door hung as straight as if she had just reached out and lightly tapped the edge to adjust it. The dressing table and bench were right where she had left them for me.

# 47

It's April 2020, and I'm not sure how many drafts of *Child* I've written, how many revisions I've gone through. Too many to only now be discovering the heart of the story.

I'm on the phone with another writer, with whom I've swapped manuscripts. She has read this memoir and is giving me feedback. She offhandedly mentions something about Mattie being just a child when she gave birth to Minnie. I don't comment. She assumes I know this. After all, I'm the author of the manuscript.

My stomach does one of those flips. That tightening deep inside. But my writer friend is on her way to making a totally different point, so I act as though I'm moving right along with her.

We end up talking for over an hour—about the reliability and fallibility of memory, about love, what it looks like, about triangles, relationships between people who are not the same family, race, or class. About what it means to be a mother. About raising a child and loving a child and are those two different things.

I thank her and we hang up. I sit at the dining room table, the pages of this memoir and the notes I've taken over the years spread before me. I begin searching for numbers. The numbers that will show how old Mattie was when she gave birth to Minnie.

The date of Mattie's birth: February 26, 1918.

The date of Minnie's birth: November 28, 1933.

*Mattie was fifteen years old when she became a mother!*

I never knew.

Well, I just never paid attention.

The equation is clear before me. It has been the entire time I've been working on this book. It's been clear before me practically my whole life. I just didn't see it. Maybe this is not so surprising, given the way a white child would not know much about the Black woman who took care of her. Maybe it's not so surprising that I didn't see it while writing this book, given my loose relationship with numbers. How my eyes glide over them.

Now I'm concentrating on Mattie's birth date and Minnie's birth date.

Exactly nine months before Minnie was born, Mattie turned fifteen. Which means it's possible Mattie became pregnant at the age of fourteen. Fifteen, the oldest she could have been.

Why didn't Mattie tell me? Thousands of days and hours we spent together, the times we were side by side, talking, talking. She never said a word about this. Of course, as a child, I could not have understood. But there were many years I thought of us as peers. Did she consider telling me, but was afraid that if I knew, I'd feel upset for her? Was she sparing me? That would not be unusual. There are always things a mother—or a person who mothers— would not want a child to know. Would not put on a child. Was it that she was too embarrassed to tell me? Was this part of her history too painful for her? Had she buried the memory so deep she could not retrieve it?

Or were we just not close enough for her to share this intimate detail? This is the explanation that is hardest for me to bear. How well did I really know her?

I picture my granddaughter, fifteen years old now—Mattie's age those nine months she was round with a baby. A rump, the oval of a baby's elbow, a chin.

*How* did she become pregnant? I don't want to acknowledge the most likely way.

An answer can open up a well of questions.

I glance through the French doors leading to our terrace. Dusk is closing in. Somewhere out there are stars ready to pop out. How long have I been sitting here?

My back is to the three-tiered, mahogany rack that used to hang over the Victorian sofa in our living room on Eden Terrace. Mother's collection of cups and saucers, some chipped, filled the shelves then. Over the years, I've removed one cup and saucer, then another, on and on, until there are only the six I love best. The rest of the shelves are now filled with books. Not so old-lady-looking this way. I remember how Mattie used to lift each cup and saucer from the shelves, place them on a big, straight-sided tray, take them into the kitchen, fill the sink with soapy water, swish the cups and saucers. One by one, she'd scoop them up and place them upside down on a dishtowel to dry. I sat at the chrome-and-Formica table in the kitchen, and together, we debated each cup and saucer, its pale shade of pink or yellow or lavender, a scalloped saucer, the shape of a cup. Finally, we picked our favorite. Always, the navy-blue square cup and its navy-blue, petal-like saucer. It was, by far, the smallest cup and saucer, and the only one that was not a pastel color. We both loved the deep blue, the unexpected.

---

I walk into my office, sit down at my rolltop desk, the last gift my father gave me, where I've worked on this memoir for three years. I pick up the phone and call Pernettia. She recently turned ninety-two. Her mind is as sharp as it was when she was crossing our backyard, taking the stairs two at a time, standing in the doorway, making Mattie laugh so hard she nearly fell off the cane-bottomed chair.

We chat a bit. Pernettia gave up driving a few months ago. Her son, Robert, and his wife, Berdell, moved closer to her. Other than her arthritis, she feels fine. I fill her in on my family. Then I say I have a question for her. Okay, she says, go ahead. During the years I've worked on this book, I've called her a number of times to ask for information. She always has answers. I swallow hard.

"So, I'm wondering, how old was Mattie when she gave birth to Minnie?"

"Oh, goodness, Judy, she was fifteen! Just a child!"

"Pernettia! I never knew that!"

"I know, I know. Mattie wouldn't want you to know."

*She wouldn't want me to know. This person I was so close with wouldn't want me to know.*

I'm quiet for a moment, roll my chair back a little from the desk. Then I say, "Was Jay Minnie's father?"

"No, no, Jay was not. I never knew who Minnie's daddy was. You know Minnie didn't look like Mattie *or* Jay. I figure her daddy was light skinned, since Minnie was so light skinned. Mattie gave Minnie to her older brother and his wife to raise right after Minnie was born."

"Right after she was born? Why?"

"Well, Mattie was too young to raise a child. And it would've ruined her reputation. Having a baby so young."

"She didn't give up raising Minnie so she could come work for us?"

"Oh no! Minnie was living with her aunt and uncle way before Mattie ever came to your mama and daddy. Minnie was living with her aunt and uncle way before Mattie married Jay. But Jay ran the streets. He should've stayed single if that's what he wanted. Oh, he was bad. Drank something awful. Wrecked his car. He could get real mean. Mattie was afraid of him. She wanted to live with your family because she was protected there. And she wanted certain things for Minnie. Minnie was smart. And when she wanted to go to college, Mattie's brother said they couldn't afford it. Mattie put her through college."

I want to ask the obvious question, but I'm not sure I should. Would it be rude? Intrusive? Would it sound as though I'm digging for dirt? I swallow hard again.

"Pernettia, I can't imagine Mattie had a boyfriend when she was fourteen."

"No, she wouldn't have had a boyfriend at that age, not out there in the country. Somebody just took advantage of that child."

I draw a long, heavy breath. Roll my chair around so that I face the family photographs covering the wall over the couch. My eyes focus on a 1979 picture of Mattie, in a lavender silk dress and dark lavender cardigan, seated in a chair in Brenda's living room, surrounded by Laurie and Mike and David, Brian, Scott, and Danny. The picture was taken at Danny's Saturday night bar-mitzvah party. Mattie would've been sixty-one.

"Oh, Pernettia," I say.

When she speaks again, her voice sounds far away: "Well, that's just the way it was."

Silence.

I change the subject: "What do you know about Mattie's parents?"

"Mattie didn't talk about her family, her mama or her daddy. Good, bad, she never did say. She was so wrapped up in y'all's family. Y'all were her family. She was just at home with y'all. That's all she wanted to talk about."

---

Sitting at my desk in my office, hearing about Mattie and Minnie, in this shadowy light, between day and night, I feel the ache of something ending and something beginning. I want to tell Pernettia everything I'm feeling. I want to thank her for still being alive. I want to thank her for being honest with me. I want to thank her for being Mattie's friend. I want to say how sad I am that Mattie never told me this monumental thing. I want to ask if she believes it defined Mattie. But most of all, I want to say how sad I am. I want to say maybe my sadness is because I was not given the chance to come up with words to comfort Mattie, words that might acknowledge how she lost her childhood but gave me mine, all while she was giving her own daughter a future.

I try to picture Mattie the age my granddaughter is now, in the ninth grade. I imagine Mattie going to school. Walking with her brothers and sisters down a dirt road, past farmland and cows and front yard chickens. Then, not at school. Did the teacher ask why she quit? Did it matter to anyone that her lessons ended?

I imagine Mattie holding a child on her hip. The child is Minnie. The child is me. You know how, in a dream, one person blurs into another. Now it's Minnie. Now it's me. We're blurred by Mattie's love—the whole known, unknowable, boundless, bound span of it.

*Mattie and me at her birthday party on our screened porch, 1981.*
*Photograph courtesy of Judy Goldman.*

# Acknowledgments

This is my favorite part of writing a book because it means I get to think about everyone who stood with me as I plugged away. A writer's job can be lonely—all those hours trying to decide whether to use a semi-colon or a dash or whether to just split the darned thing into two separate sentences. Truth is, I never feel lonely, because I'm a lucky soul who has good and gracious people rooting for me.

Let's start with family, and husband Henry—for over five decades, my everything. Any book I write is because he encouraged me to write it. Gratitude is not a big enough word for my daughter and son-in-law, Laurie (who helped me so much with this book) and Bob Smithwick; my son and daughter-in-law, Mike and Brooke Goldman. They cheer me on every day. I wish you could meet them; you'd fall in love with them. You'd also love my grandchildren—Lucy and Zoe Smithwick, Tess and Benjamin Goldman. I could spend pages just telling you how amazing they are. In loving memory of my parents, Peggy and Ben Kurtz, who'd be thrilled to see a book about Mattie. In loving memory of my sister, Brenda Meltsner. Love to my brother, Donald Kurtz. And to nephews, nieces, cousins, sister-in-law—Brian and Tonya Meltsner, Scott Meltsner and Lisa McCloud, Danny and Diana Meltsner, Jeff and Sherry Cohen, Doug and Ashli Cohen, 'Leen Cohen, Adam Cohen and Cooper Heins, Sasha and Dave Koren, Tracy Seretean, Debbie and Mike Rubin, Charlotte and Alan Kahn, Betty Roth, Mara Kurtz.

Gratitude to Pernettia Rowell, who shares my memories and, in her nineties, fills in when I forget. Gratitude to Mattie's grand-daughters, Michelle Callender Diggs, Linda Callender Williams, and Lauren Callender Hightower, for providing details and trusting me with their grandmother's story. In grateful memory of Minnie Callender, their mother.

Gratitude to my breakfast group and dear friends—Bobbie Campbell, Ann Haskell, Laurie Johnston, Dannye Powell, Trisha Schwabacher. Mary Fenster, Beth Kephart, Judy Pera, Marilyn Perlman, Kathryne Perrill, Paula Reckson, Betsy Rock. Table Rock Writers' Workshop, especially Georgann Eubanks and Donna Campbell. Jonathan Haupt and Joseph Bathanti, big-hearted pals. Gratitude to Denny Gallis for all he gave me before I narrowed the focus of this book.

Great gratitude to my dream agent, Grainne Fox at Fletcher & Co. She's the kind of agent who isn't supposed to exist any more—hardworking, kind, incredibly generous with her time and expertise. Who else do you know who uses the word *nobble*?

Speaking of dream people to work with—Aurora Bell, acquisitions editor at University of South Carolina Press, also belongs in that category. She's talented, efficient, warm, and delightful. The entire University of South Carolina Press is wonderful to be in cahoots with. The perfect home for my memoir. Richard Brown, director; Pat Callahan, editorial, design, and production director; MacKenzie Collier, director of publicity and strategic partnerships; Kerri Tolan, production editor; Kemi Ogunji, marketing and design coordinator; and Ida Audeh, copyeditor—thank you.

Early readers of this manuscript, now I'm talking about you: Abigail DeWitt's guidance shaped just about every page. Darnell Arnoult, Betsy Thorpe, Dana Sachs, Dannye Powell, Maya Myers, Stephanie Whetstone, Paul Austin—careful readers all.

Gratitude to our independent bookstores, who encourage writers and take good care of readers (especially Charlotte's own Park Road Books). Gratitude to our town's splendid literary community —fellow writers, workshop students, and organizers (especially Charlotte Lit's Kathie Collins and Paul Reali).

Gratitude to the Women's National Book Association for selecting an excerpt from this memoir as a finalist in their 2020 Flash Nonfiction contest.

———

I changed the names of some people to disguise their identity and protect their privacy. If I could not recall a minor detail (a piece of dialogue, for example), I tried to, at least, capture the spirit.